Young Pathfinder 6

A CILT series for primary language teachers

Let's join in!

Finger and action rhymes

Cynthia Martin
with Catherine Cheater

CiLT The National Centre for Languages

The publisher and authors acknowledge with thanks the copyright-holders who have granted permission to reproduce illustrations and texts extracted from their work. A list of these is provided on p66. The authors have been collecting rhymes, songs and traditional verses, mainly verbally from FLAs and native speakers in the classroom, for several years. They have, as far as possible, endeavoured to acknowledge sources but this has not always been possible. The publisher would therefore be glad to hear from any such unacknowledged copyright-holders.

The authors would like thank Bernice Culley for her ideas for the finger clicking alternative for the days of the week (p8) and for the ABC clapping sequence (p35). They would also like to thank Marc Padellec of CILT for his design and typographic contribution to the book.

First published 1998 by the Centre for Information on Language Teaching and Research, 20 Bedfordbury, Covent Garden, London WC2N 4LB.

ISBN 1 902031 09 1

A catalogue record for this book is available from the British Library

Cover design by Neil Alexander.
Printed in the United Kingdom by Hobbs the Printers Ltd, Totton, Hampshire SO40 3WX

CILT Publications are available from: **Central Books,** 99 Wallis Rd, London E9 5LN. Tel: 0845 458 9910. Fax: 0845 458 9912. Book trade representation (UK and Ireland): **Broadcast Book Services,** Charter House, 27a London Road, Croydon CR0 2RE. Tel: 020 8681 8949. Fax: 020 8688 0615.

Contents

Introduction

This Young Pathfinder is intended as a practical resource for both specialist and non-specialist teachers of French and German at primary level, and for teachers at Key Stage 3 who would like ideas to supplement their coursebook. It brings together within one publication a collection of rhymes, poems and songs which have proved motivating for learners from three to thirteen. It will also provide teachers of lesser taught languages with ideas which they can adapt to their own needs.

However, this is more than an anthology. Alongside each set of rhymes and songs there are either instructions in English or illustrations which suggest possible strategies for presenting the rhymes. The collection is divided into two parts.

Part 1 contains examples which are most suited to young children, from pre-school through Key Stage 1 to beginning learners at Key Stage 2, and which can be spoken to help children master the pronunciation of new sound clusters. Although the suggestions all promote listening and speaking and require no reading of words, initial literacy and numeracy skills are developed and reinforced in both the mother tongue and the foreign language.

Part 2 contains ideas for working with older children in Key Stages 2 and 3, using simple texts to introduce language topics through rhymes and songs suitable for children with growing reading and writing skills. We also suggest a number of short poems which we have found especially suitable for illustration and copywriting and for linking with ongoing topics in the primary classroom.

There are suggestions for taking the language further for those of you working with more able pupils or with the need to differentiate within the classroom. The theme of classroom language is revisited with further ideas for creating your own rhymes to promote independent pupil use of the target language, especially when playing simple games.

Both parts contain examples of traditional foreign language rhymes and songs which will provide an opportunity for introducing pupils to aspects of the foreign culture and for celebrating linguistic and cultural diversity.

Although our examples are generally grouped thematically, throughout our main purpose has been to demonstrate how oracy and literacy skills can be promoted and enhanced both in and through the foreign language.

Why rhymes, poems and songs?

We start with a few thoughts about why we use foreign language rhymes, poems and songs in our regular teaching repertoire. Reciting rhymes and learning songs:

- continue the kinds of activities with which many children are familiar from pre-school groups;

- involve children in active learning and appeal to all the senses;

- are a natural way for children to learn;

- enhance oracy, literacy and numeracy work in the mother tongue by helping children develop listening and speaking skills and more accurate pronunciation;

- help children respond to rhythmical patterns in language (both the foreign language and their L1) and recognise rhyme;

- can be adapted to suit different areas of language;

- can help to teach or reinforce gender, syntax and sophisticated language structures 'painlessly';

- allow children to reproduce language with confidence and fluency;

- enable children to compare versions of rhymes from both Britain and abroad;

- broaden children's knowledge about language and their awareness and cultural diversity; and most of all

- rhymes, poems and songs are enjoyable and **memorable.**

2 — Young Pathfinder 6: *Let's join in! Rhymes, poems and songs*

CiLT

PART 1
Starting Off: Key Stage 1 and beginners

As soon as children are able to participate in communicative activities, they are able to begin learning a foreign language. If the class teacher has the confidence to include some foreign language activities in the daily planning, together with sufficient competence in the chosen language, the children are likely to accept the foreign language as a normal part of what goes on in school.

Rhymes and songs make an important contribution to the overall language development of the child as they instil into the learner's mind a sense of the rhythm of the language and its sentence patterns. If the child is able to learn by heart and recite, then the ability to articulate and enunciate particular sounds has been mastered too. Rhymes and songs in the mother tongue are therefore strongly recommended.

But how and why should the Key Stage 1 class teacher introduce rhymes, poems and songs in a foreign language? The 'how' is explained throughout this book, in easy, progressive steps, by means of activities which help to build self-esteem, contributing to the child's ability to concentrate and listen, to speak fluently and articulately and ultimately, to the development of literacy skills.

It is the **frequency of exposure** to the foreign language which is far more important than the **length of time spent**. This is particularly true when your children are of nursery age or at Key Stage 1. Therefore, we recommend including an activity in the foreign language every day, even if only for one or two minutes. Five minutes of **planned** activity in the foreign language every day would be ideal. Once a small repertoire of rhymes and songs has been built up, five minutes will allow for several items to be covered, and this can become part of the daily routine of the class.

The suggestions that follow are not a scheme of work. They are parcels of activities which you can incorporate into your own programme as suits your personal needs. Where possible we have tried to arrange the rhymes and songs to suit different topics that you are likely to be teaching but the order in which you tackle different items is flexible. However, throughout we have tried to indicate various principles that are important to bear in mind, even if you are dipping in and out of this resource.

The following rhymes and songs can be used within the classroom, with children sitting at tables, standing at their desks or on the carpet. Some require no movement around the room, and others require slightly more space. The first ones we suggest are particularly **suitable for regular use, as part of the classroom 'routine'**, to be said over and over again, whenever there is a suitable moment.

 ### RHYMES TO SAY

We begin with **spoken rhymes** which are a good place to start if you have not had much experience as yet of using foreign language rhymes. Spoken rhymes have the advantage of no music or tunes to be learned. Both you and the children can concentrate on the words and actions.

GREETINGS

Here are some **finger rhymes** for beginners in French and German. For these, the children can stay in their places, as they are moving fingers or upper body only. They are based on the daily greetings which can be taught early on and practised every day. Start off by going round greeting the children saying '*bonjour/Hallo/Guten Morgen*' to each with a handshake. Then go to the door and wave 'goodbye' with the words '*au revoir/Auf Wiedersehen*'. Children are likely to begin echoing what you are saying almost at once. Next introduce the following little rhyme:

	make a fist
Bonjour Papa!	put up thumb
Bonjour Maman!	raise forefinger
Bonjour mon frère!	middle finger
Bonjour ma soeur!	ringfinger
Et moi	little finger
Bonjour petit (doigt!)	wave whole hand to get attention

You can stop at this point. When your learners are ready, you can continue by reversing the process:

Au revoir Papa!	put down thumb
Au revoir Maman!	put down forefinger
Au revoir mon frère!	put down middle finger
Au revoir ma soeur!	put down fourth finger
Et moi	speak to little finger
Au revoir petit (doigt!)	wave with other hand as you say 'goodbye'
	finish with fingers in a fist once more

CiLT

Bear in mind the principle, **frequent exposure** to the foreign language for **short bursts every day**. This helps embed the pattern and sound of the foreign language in the children's minds, in the same way in which it is widely believed that mother tongue nursery rhymes need to be, in order for the child to become a competent speaker and reader.

The next rhyme introduces the important word '*voici*' which you will need over and over again, when presenting new vocabulary using realia or visuals. Note how the rhyme also **re-uses** the word '*doigt*' from the previous example, so the children are working with a rhyme in which some of the expressions are already familiar. **What is fresh is being introduced in tiny bite-size 'chunks'.**

Voici ma main	hold up one hand
Voici mes doigts	wiggle fingers
Petit pouce cache-toi	tuck little finger away
Au revoir!	wave goodbye with other hand

If you wish, you can extend the activity further by continuing with another rhyme using the expression '*toc! toc! toc!*' for 'knock, knock, knock'.

Toc! Toc! Toc!	knock gently on fist three times.
Petit pouce. *Es-tu là?*	whisper
Chut!	finger to lips
Je dors	head on hands to feign sleep

You can substitute other words for '*Petit pouce*', for example '*M. Pouce, Mme Pouce*', or the name of a teddy, toy, animal or child in the class.

Possibilities in German are as follows:

Eine Hand,	show one hand
zwei Hände,	two hands
der Daumen,	show thumb
der Zeigefinger,	index finger
der Mittelfinger,	middle finger
der Ringfinger,	fourth finger
der kleine Finger.	little finger

You can then add in the greetings you have been practising. Start by making a fist.

Hallo/guten Morgen, Daumen!	raise thumb
Hallo, Zeigefinger!	raise index finger
Hallo, Mittelfinger!	middle finger
Hallo, Ringfinger!	fourth finger
Hallo, kleiner Finger!	wave with one hand

Reverse the process when appropriate:

Tschüs, Daumen!	fold down thumb
Tschüs, Zeigefinger!	index finger
Tschüs, Mittelfinger!	middle finger
Tschüs, Ringfinger!	fourth finger
Tschüs, kleiner Finger!	little finger
	wave with one hand

All these rhymes are quick and easy to learn because they are short and linked to clear finger actions. They can be repeated often and involve all children, including those who are more orally reticent, because they can join in with the actions immediately and take part in the speaking when they are ready. Try to incorporate these into a regular routine. And when everyone is familiar with these, ring the changes by trying another traditional finger rhyme.

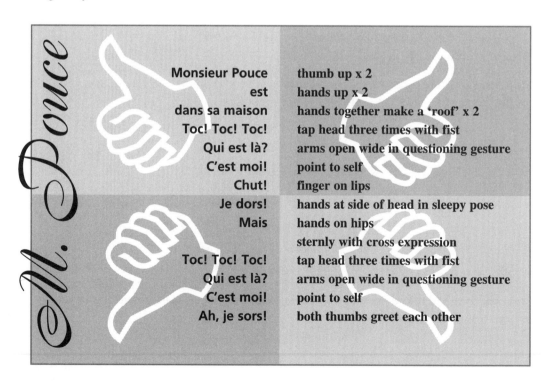

Monsieur Pouce	**thumb up x 2**
est	**hands up x 2**
dans sa maison	**hands together make a 'roof' x 2**
Toc! Toc! Toc!	**tap head three times with fist**
Qui est là?	**arms open wide in questioning gesture**
C'est moi!	**point to self**
Chut!	**finger on lips**
Je dors!	**hands at side of head in sleepy pose**
Mais	**hands on hips**
	sternly with cross expression
Toc! Toc! Toc!	**tap head three times with fist**
Qui est là?	**arms open wide in questioning gesture**
C'est moi!	**point to self**
Ah, je sors!	**both thumbs greet each other**

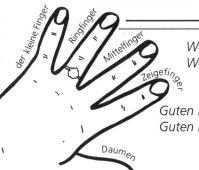

Here is a similar rhyme in German:

Wo ist der Daumen?

Wo ist der Daumen?	both hands out, thumbs hidden in fist
Wo ist der Daumen?	
Hier bin ich!	one thumb pops up
Hier bin ich!	other thumb pops up
Guten Morgen, Daumen!	wiggle one thumb at a time
Guten Morgen, Daumen!	thumbs 'greet' each other
Weg ist er!	turn hands into fists
Weg ist er!	one at a time

Children will become comfortable with the language if the same rhymes are revisited regularly, as with English nursery rhymes which children enjoy singing again and again. The impact is created because of the regularity with which the children join in.

Still on the greetings theme we next suggest some **rhymes with actions.**

Guten Morgen, guten Morgen,	children stand up and shake hands
wir winken uns zu!	children wave to each other
Guten Morgen, guten Morgen,	children sit down
erst ich und dann du!	teacher waves, then children wave back

Linked with greetings you may probably be adding the expression '*ça va?*' with a 'thumbs up' signal and '*oui, ça va*' response. You can then introduce this 'home-made' rhyme. You will notice that the actions which accompany the words are simple, fairly large movements which are very straightforward to remember and to do.

Lundi matin	
Lundi matin	stand up
Bonjour, ça va?	shake hands with partner
Lundi soir	sit down
Au revoir!	wave goodbye to partner

DAYS OF THE WEEK

You can say the above rhyme each morning, substituting the appropriate day of the week. To teach the days of the week you can combine the words for each day with simple actions along the following lines. The first starts from a sitting position and finishes with the children all standing. The second alternative can be done either seated or standing, and gives suggestions for making clapping movements and finger clicking if the children can manage these! Whatever movements you choose, it is the combination of actions to accompany the speaking which helps the new words 'stick' in the mind.

Lundi	hands on lap	**or**	click fingers left hand x2
Mardi	hands on shoulders		click fingers right x2
Mercredi	touch your ears		click fingers both hands
Jeudi	touch your nose		touch left elbow
Vendredi	hands on head		touch right elbow
Samedi	hands in the air		clap together
Dimanche	stand up		clap over head

A game can evolve from this activity. When everyone is familiar with the words and actions, call out a day of the week and the pupils must do the action. Start by giving the verbal cue and getting the children to respond with the appropriate action. In this way, the children are showing you that they understand but without needing to produce the foreign language. You could even do this as an elimination game if suitable for your group.

Later, when pupils are confident, they can call out the words instead of you. Stand close by to the volunteer so you can whisper a prompt if need be! And if the children are ready to do so, you can reverse the procedure and perform the action to elicit the day of the week, but this is more difficult.

Children will be swept along singing the days of the week in this specially composed song in which each day is echoed. They do not need to see the written words at all.

les sept jours de la semaine, les voici x 2
lundi, lundi
mardi, mardi
mercredi, mercredi
jeudi, jeudi
vendredi, vendredi
samedi, samedi
dimanche, dimanche
C'est fini. Et allons-y!

les 7 jours

LANGUAGE OF THE CLASSROOM

Classroom language needs daily reinforcement. The following rhyme is based on **instructions** you are going to be giving throughout the day. It uses the same sitting down and getting up movements from the German greetings rhyme we started with, with a twirl at the end!

Setz dich
Setz dich!	sit down
Steh auf!	stand up
Dreh dich um! x 2	turn round twice

Introduce this by **saying the instruction** and **doing the action** for the children to copy along with you. Let the children **echo** what you are saying. Do it at **normal speed**, then **very slowly**, then **very fast**, then **whispering.** Next you can extend the activity by adding another simple action, clapping hands.

Klatsch in die Hände!	clap hands
Klatsch in die Hände!	
Setz dich!	sit down
Steh auf!	stand up
Dreh dich um!	turn round

Other commands you will need to be giving regularly can be combined with simple mimes. For example

Ecoutez	hands behind ears	*Hört zu!*
Regardez	hands on forehead 'looking'	*Seht her!*
Taisez-vous	finger to lips	*Seid still!*
Chut!	finger to lips	*Psst!*
Chut!	finger to lips	*Schhh!*

These instructions can be recited both singly and in sequence. The repeated and increasingly quiet whispering of the 'Shhh' twice at the end has the effect of focusing the children down.

As your pupils become familiar with the foreign language expressions, add others, inventing suitable gestures.

Asseyez-vous correctement!	sit up straight	*Sitzt gerade!*
Levez le doigt!	hand in air	*Meldet euch!*
Croisez les bras!	fold arms	*Arme verschränken!*
Fermez les yeux!	eyes shut	*Augen zu!*
Ouvrez les yeux!	eyes open	*Augen auf!*

CREATING YOUR OWN REPERTOIRE: RHYMES TO SING

As a next step, you can move on from rhymes to say to introducing some simple rhymes to sing. Home-made songs can be built up using familiar nursery rhyme tunes. Many children already have a store of rhymes and tunes from English which we as teachers can capitalise on, so we are now going to concentrate on different ways in which we can make these tunes the context and support for fresh learning in the foreign language. So, for example, you might remember the tune *Lavender's blue*. Write it out in English and mark the syllables. You might get something like

```
1  2  3    4    5 6 7 8
Lavender's blue, dilly dilly        8
        1  2  3    4
        Lavender's green            4
1  2  3    4    5 6 7 8
Lavender's blue, dilly dilly        8
        1    2    3    4
        You shall be Queen!         4
```

This can be adapted to become:

Tune: *Lavender's blue*	*Levez le doigt, guili guili*	8	put up your hand, tickle yourself
	Baissez le doigt	4	put down your hand
	Levez le doigt, guili guili	8	put up your hand, tickle yourself
	Croisez les bras	4	fold arms

Note how the expressions '*levez le doigt*' and '*croisez les bras*' which have been practised in spoken form, are now recycled with the new tune.

TELLING CHILDREN WHAT TO DO

You can add variety to the repetition of many instructions by singing them to a nursery rhyme tune.

Tune: *Hickory, Dickory Dock*	*Levez-vous, asseyez-vous*	stand up, sit down
	Levez-vous, asseyez-vous	
	Asseyez-vous correctement	sit up 'properly'
	Levez-vous, asseyez-vous	stand up, sit down

or even

	Ecoutez, écoutez	hands behind ears
	Regardez, regardez	hands on forehead looking
Tune: *Three blind mice*	*Asseyez-vous correctement*	sit up properly
	Asseyez-vous correctement	
	Asseyez-vous correctement	be quiet
	Taisez-vous!	

Rhymes and songs are another means of integrating the foreign language into the primary child's day. For example, throughout the primary day you will be moving children in and out of the classroom, to go to assembly, out to play, to lunch, PE, and eventually home time. All the children sing and keep repeating while the teacher points in turn to children who must join the line. This is a good way of getting everyone to line up calmly at the end of the day, or to quietly move children from the carpet to the door.

---

for getting into line . . .

Mettez-vous en ligne
Mettez-vous en ligne
Tous les enfants de la classe
Mettez-vous en ligne

Tune: *The Farmer's in his den*

You can use the **same tune for other expressions** such as:

Mettez-vous en cercle (for getting into a circle); *Ramassez les livres/cahiers/ feuilles* (for collecting books/worksheets); *Rangez vos affaires* (for packing away).

A German version fits another tune. Again you can adapt the same tune for different words:

Setzt euch im Kreise hin (for getting into a circle); *Sammelt die Bücher/Blätter ein* (for collecting books/worksheets); *Packt eure Sachen ein* (for clearing away).

---

for lining up . . .

Stellt euch hintereinander auf,
alle Kinder, alle Kinder!
Stellt euch hintereinander auf,
alle Kinder!

Tune: *Nuts in May*

And when you want the children to echo what you are saying, as you present and practise new language, you can signal you wish them to repeat after you by singing an adaptation of *Frère Jacques*.

Toute la classe
Toute la classe
Répétez
Répétez

Répétez après moi
Répétez après moi
Après moi
Après moi

Tune: *Frère Jacques*

Songs with short lines and inbuilt repetition are best for young learners.

PRAISING YOUR PUPILS

How about literally singing your children's praises using the following? Everyone can join in when someone has done something well!

Formidable, formidable,
Formidable, cher Paul/chère Jane
Formidable, formidable
Formidable, cher Paul/chère Jane

Ausgezeichnet, ausgezeichnet!
Ausgezeichnet, lieber Paul/liebe Jane!
Ausgezeichnet, ausgezeichnet!
Ausgezeichnet, lieber Paul/liebe Jane!

COUNTING

Counting in the foreign language is extremely popular with young children, and will probably be one of the first areas you tackle. It also brings with it the added advantage of giving counting practice in a different context. A good way in is to encourage the children to copy you by holding up the same number of fingers as you, and echoing what you say.

Un   *Eins*

Deux   *Zwei*

Trois   *Drei*

When the children have learned to count up to three in French or German, you can then teach them to sing a song using only those three words.

Tune: *Frère Jacques/ Bruder Jakob*		
	Un, deux, trois	Eins, zwei, drei!
	Un deux, trois	Eins, zwei, drei!
	Un, deux, trois	Eins, zwei, drei!
	Un, deux, trois	Eins, zwei, drei!

If the children always hold up the correct number of fingers to match the number they are singing, you already have your first number song.

Childhood tunes are often very flexible. Keep a list of **short tunes** with **strong intonation patterns** and the **right sort of syllable count per line**. Indicate the syllables and they will form a ready made resource bank from which to create your own songs as the need arises.

If you need to revisit these very early numbers in a slightly different way, try reciting some of these action rhymes, which also practise parts of the body. Still sitting in their places, children can move hands and feet in the next two rhymes which incorporate the first three numbers 'one, two and three'.

12 — Young Pathfinder 6: *Let's join in! Rhymes, poems and songs*

CILT

Mes petites mains font tap! Tap! Tap!	clap hands x 3
Mes petits pieds font paf! Paf! Paf!	tap feet gently on floor
Un deux trois	clap palms x 3
Un deux trois	tap feet x 3
Trois petits tours	turn hands in windmill action x 3
Et puis s'en va	hands behind backs

Klatsch in die Hände

Klatsch in die Hände, klapp, klapp, klapp!	clap hands x 3
Klatsch in die Hände, eins, zwei, drei!	clap hands x 3
Stampf mit den Füßen, trapp, trapp, trapp!	tap feet x 3
Stampf mit den Füßen, eins, zwei, drei!	tap feet x 3

Notice how the German expression '*Klatsch in die Hände*' is re-cycled from the earlier rhyme we used for class instructions, with just the addition of one more verb and one body part. These accompany the first three numbers as in the French example, which you are likely to have been teaching already.

Next, you might like to build on the numbers by counting on to 'four' and adding a rhyming line accompanied by actions. Join together in a circle and as you chant the words, encourage the children to feel the beat through their bodies and keep time with it by skipping, marching, walking to the beat, one step at a time.

Eins, zwei

Eins, zwei, drei und vier,	skipping round in circle
drei und vier, drei und vier.	skip back other way
Eins, zwei, drei und vier,	change direction
gib mir die Hand und tanz mit mir!	join hands and swing partner

When you have taken the children further in their counting, you can sing the numbers one to **seven** to another well-known tune. **Do not feel obliged to limit your counting to blocks of five or ten.**

Un, deux, trois, quatre, cinq, six, sept
or
Eins, zwei, drei, vier, fünf, sechs, sieben

Tune: *Twinkle twinkle little star*

As the original nursery rhyme has six lines, you will have encouraged the children to count up to seven six times quite painlessly! This can still be an action song if the children hold up the correct number of fingers to match each number.

When you want the children to follow the song text in a different way, you could make a large song sheet with the numbers represented for instance by domino style symbols.

If you would like the children to recognise and follow the number symbols, you can produce a song text for them to 'read' as they sing:

1   2   3   4   5   6   7

Voici 🤚 ma main 🖐
Elle a 🤚 cinq doigts 🖐
En voici 🖐 En voici 🖐

Now you can go back to your finger rhymes and re-use the numbers in another context. Here is the traditional rhyme *Voici ma main*. You will see that it **recycles previously learned language**, both the phrase '*voici ma main*' and the word '*doigt*' re-occur from earlier finger rhymes.

With young learners **counting aloud** is a necessary tool to aid children's development in **numeracy.** Rhymes and songs with a counting element in the foreign language not only teach the foreign language numbers but also serve to reinforce the number concepts being introduced in English. The next rhyme is a good one for getting children to count along with you. Draw an Eiffel Tower on the board and then count up the rungs of the ladder with your fingers as high as you need to go for the stage of your learners. Count as high as suits your class.

La Tour Eiffel
A 300 mètres
Pour y aller
Faut une échelle
1, 2, 3, 4, etc

As we demonstrated above, you can adapt a well-known tune such as *Frère Jacques* to build up very **early counting sequences.** Use the same tune, but instead of limiting yourself to the numbers 1–3, you gradually move on through 4–6, 7–9 and finally to 10. The French version has the neat rhyme between '*six*' and '*dix*' at the end, but the German version is still possible. This is how it goes:

Tune: *Frère Jacques*				Tune: *Bruder Jakob*
Un, deux, trois	**1**	**2**	**3**	*Eins, zwei, drei,*
Un, deux, trois	**1**	**2**	**3**	*eins, zwei, drei.*
Quatre, cinq, six	**4**	**5**	**6**	*Vier, fünf, sechs,*
Quatre, cinq, six	**4**	**5**	**6**	*vier, fünf, sechs.*
Sept, huit, neuf	**7**	**8**	**9**	*Sieben, acht, neun,*
Sept, huit, neuf	**7**	**8**	**9**	*sieben, acht, neun.*
Dix, dix, dix	**10**	**10**	**10**	*Zehn, zehn, zehn,*
Dix, dix, dix	**10**	**10**	**10**	*zehn, zehn, zehn.*

If you are teaching French it is possible to follow a similar pattern when your class is ready to add on the next sequence from eleven to twenty. In this way, the children have the security of re-using the early numbers, and the sense of progression as they gradually add in the later ones.

Onze, douze, treize	11	12	13
Onze, douze, treize	11	12	13
Quatorze, quinze	14	15	
Quatorze, quinze	14	15	
Seize, dix-sept, dix-huit	16	17	18
Seize, dix-sept, dix-huit	16	17	18
Dix-neuf, vingt	19	20	
Dix-neuf, vingt	19	20	

If your children are already able to recognise numbers in their actual form, these can constitute the song text visually, and you can hold up number cards or write figures 1–10 or 1–20 on the board. If not, then for songs up to ten, the correct number of fingers can be held up.

Another well-known English nursery rhyme tune you can adapt for counting purposes is *Ten little indians*. For example you could substitute the noun 'indian (boys)' with a pet or animal with a 'two-syllable' foreign language name.

Un petit, deux petits, trois petits lapins
Quatre petits, cinq petits, six petits lapins
Sept petits, huit petits, neuf petits lapins
Dix petits lapins sautent.

Tune: *Ten little indians*

At Key Stage 1 you can simply sing the first verse, choosing whatever pet fits the pattern. Later on, as children progress, they can learn other verses, each time substituting one noun plus an appropriate verb:

un petit, deux petits
trois petits **oiseaux**

. . .

dix petits oiseaux
volent

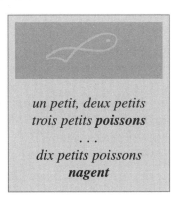

un petit, deux petits
trois petits **poissons**

. . .

dix petits poissons
nagent

un petit, deux petits
trois petits **nounours**

. . .

dix petits nounours
dorment

Perhaps a good suggestion to close with!

AUTHENTIC COUNTING OUT RHYMES

Next we continue with some **'counting out'** rhymes which you can use when **choosing** a pupil to do something. To begin with we are recycling the numbers one to seven only.

Une oie
Une oie
Deux oies
Trois oies
Quatre oies
Cinq oies
Six oies
Sept oies (C'est toi!)
(point to each child
as you say each line)

This rhyme takes learners a step further as far as '*neuf*':

Une pomme
Une pomme
Deux pommes
Trois pommes
Quatre pommes
Cinq pommes

Six pommes
Sept pommes
Huit pommes
Pont neuf
Queue d'boeuf!

And still on the 'apple' theme here is a rhyme for you to introduce when you are presenting **colours.** You could use plastic fruit, with the golden apple appropriately painted, or coloured pictures, or two real red and green apples to show. Both magazines and storybooks are good sources.

LA POMME VERTE

Une pomme verte
Une pomme rouge
Une pomme d'or
C'est toi qui est dehors!

RAISING CULTURAL AWARENESS

Here is a 'counting out' rhyme also incorporating the colours red and green to be said around **Easter time**. Learning it could be linked to a little information about the German custom of painting Easter eggs and making hanging decorations. You can tell your class that on Easter Sunday morning either Easter eggs or painted eggs are hidden in the garden which the Easter bunny *(der Osterhase)* is supposed to have placed there. Children have great fun going out and collecting the eggs and placing them in little Easter nests they have made for the purpose. You might like to make your own Easter nest for the classroom and search for miniature eggs with wrappings in bright colours. Seeking for these in response to the instructions *'Bring mir ein rotes/grünes/blaues/gelbes Ei'* (and of course eating them afterwards!) would be a popular way to revise colours!

In dem grünen Gras   Legt ein rotes Ei

Sitzt ein kleiner Has   Und du bist frei!

NONSENSE RHYMES

There are several 'counting out' rhymes with 'nonsense' words which you can teach like tongue twisters.

(note that for this one, every syllable is counting out a person)

Am stram gram

Am stram gram
Pic et pic et colegram
Bourre et bourre et ratatam
*Am stram **gram***

Whoever is picked out on this last syllable is eliminated and then the rhyme begins again. Point with your finger very definitely to each child as each syllable is spoken emphatically. The same applies to these rhymes in German.

Eene, meene, miste,
es rappelt in der Kiste.
Eene, meene, meck,
*und du bist **weg!***

Ich und du,
Müllers Kuh,
Müllers Esel,
*das bist **du!***

These rhymes can be used not only with the children being counted out. With young learners who have difficulty waiting their 'turn' it can be more enjoyable to line up four of the cuddly toys, puppets or dolls to be counted. The whole class can then recite the *'am stram gram'* or *'eene meene miste'* three times in order to find the chosen toy. This keeps everyone involved.

Don't forget that many children will love to rise to the challenge of 'showing' these nonsense rhymes and jingles, as a class or in small groups, to an audience. But of course, no one should ever be pressurised.

FAVOURITE PRIMARY TOPICS

COLOURS

Still on the theme of colours, if you prefer more traditional rhymes and songs, here is one incorporating just two colours and repetitive movements. There is a **firm beat** and the **actions are repeated.**

Pomme de reinette

x x Pomme de reinette	clenched fists one on top of the other
x x Et pomme d'api	swap hands on each beat (x)
x x Tapis, tapis	both hands tap on table with knuckles
x x Rouge	tap on table, palms upwards
x x Pomme de reinette	clenched fists one on top of the other
x x Et pomme d'api	
x x Tapis, tapis	both hands tap on table with knuckles
x Gris	tap on table, palms upward

When using the foreign language to help young children differentiate between various colours, it is helpful to have some visual props to hand which clearly show the meaning of what is being sung. These props can be:

- a set of crayons/felt tip pens/chalks (large enough to be seen by all the children in the class);
- a set of coloured cards/sticky paper, tissue or crepe paper squares or strips;
- multi link cubes;
- scissors with coloured handles;
- any coloured equipment you have to hand in the primary classroom.

Hold up these cues to to indicate which colour is being mentioned.

For those of you teaching German, here is a rhyme to introduce some of the colours of the rainbow. You can point the colours out on a big picture of a rainbow, or introduce the rhyme when you are painting and have the paints to hand. When you are not doing art, you can give out coloured cards for red, orange, yellow, green and blue, and the children can stand up when their colour is mentioned. If you distribute several sets of cards around the class, you will have four or five children springing to their feet or waving their card when their colour is called. This involves more children simultaneously and keeps up their interest.

The rainbow rhyme can be done as a spoken activity, and gestures can accompany '*Ein Regenbogen*' and '*komm und schau!*'

Der Regenbogen

Ein Regenbogen	big arm movements in rainbow shape
Komm und schau	hand over eyes 'looking'
Rot, orange	children with colour cards
Gelb, grün und blau!	wave them, etc

It can also be sung.
Here is the notation:

Alternatively, let us imagine you are adapting *Frère Jacques* for colours instead. You could hold up a blue, red, green and yellow pair of children's scissors and sing:

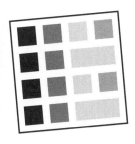

Tune: *Frère Jacques*	Tune: *Bruder Jakob*
Bleu rouge vert jaune	*Blau, rot, gelb, grün,*
Bleu rouge vert jaune	*blau, rot, gelb, grün.*
Bleu rouge vert	*Blau, rot, gelb,*
Bleu rouge vert	*blau, rot, gelb.*
Bleu rouge vert jaune	*Blau, rot, gelb, grün,*
Bleu rouge vert jaune	*blau, rot, gelb, grün.*
Bleu rouge vert	*Blau, rot, gelb,*
Bleu rouge vert	*blau, rot, gelb.*

Here the visual representation of the 'song text' is achieved by arranging pieces of coloured card or paper in the desired order. It is very important to **place the visual prompts in the reading direction, in order to develop and reinforce basic literacy skills**, helping children to see that 'words' are read from left to right and from top to bottom. (illustration missing)

This is a supportive way of encouraging learners in Key Stage 1 to 'read' a visual text. You will notice that the long held note at the end of the second and fourth lines to which we sing '*vert*' or '*gelb*' is represented by a **longer strip of colour** indicating to the children that they have to hold this note for longer.

MONTHS

As well as the days of the week, you may wish to introduce the months of the year. The first rhyme is teacher devised and helps children memorise the sequence of the months. As the foreign language names are fairly similar to the English, children are usually quick to pick them up. This rhyme practises animals as well, which happen to have been represented by soft toys in the classroom already!

Janvier, février, mars

Janvier, février, mars, avril
Perroquet et crocodile
Mai, juin, juillet, août
Perroquet, crocodile et mammouth
Septembre, octobre, novembre, décembre
Pommes de terre en robe de chambre!   Jacket potatoes!

One way of practising the months of the year could be to make a simple flip book, with a picture for each month on each page, for example a Christmas tree for December, a snowman for January, an umbrella for April, a bucket and spade for August. For February, which features in the next rhyme, you could stick on a brightly coloured 'heart' shape to go with Valentine's Day. You could then combine reciting the months with another theme which recurs in the primary classroom, that of the **weather.**

Februar

Der zweite Monat im Jahr,	hold up two fingers
das ist der Monat Februar.	'draw' big heart shape with hands
Die Sonne scheint,	make big circle gesture
der Schnee, der fällt.	make snow falling gestures with fingers in air
Lustig ist die ganze Welt!	Dance on the spot

Alternatively, you could 'cue' the rhyme line by line by getting children to hold up visuals: a '2' for the first line, a 'heart' for *Februar*, a big weather picture of the sun and of the snow for the next two lines, and a 'smiley' face for the last line. As the visuals are held up, the appropriate line is said altogether.

Another well-known tune which can be adapted to practise the months is *Jingle bells*.

Tune: *Jingle bells*	*Janvier, février,* *Mars, avril et mai* *Juin, juillet*	*Août, septembre* *Octobr(e), novembr(e)* *Décembr(e)*

Again this song is based round a tune **already familiar to the children and you in English. This means that everyone can concentrate on the new words and the tune takes care of itself.** Do not overload children with too many new tasks to perform. It is actually very tricky getting your tongue round new foreign language words, having to try to remember them, **and** fit them to a tune you do not know. So if you borrow a tune already known you can all **focus on one new set of things at a time.**

BIRTHDAYS

Birthdays are always tremendously significant for children and a natural talking point when you are learning the months, so we suggest adapting *Happy birthday*.

Tune: *Happy birthday*

Joyeux Anniversaire	*Zum Geburtstag viel Glück!*
Joyeux Anniversaire	*Zum Geburtstag viel Glück!*
Joyeux Anniversaire	*Zum Geburtstag, zum Geburtstag,*
Joyeux Anniversaire	*zum Geburtstag viel Glück!*

WEATHER AND SEASONS

Linked with the months are weather and seasons, so we continue with some traditional action rhymes which fit in with this topic. The actions performed while saying the rhyme help embed the meaning.

Es tropft.	hands up and down in air	drizzle
Es regnet.	finger tips tap on table top	rain
Es hagelt.	with flats of fingers	hail
Es gießt.	tap louder and faster	pouring
Es donnert.	hammer with fists	thunder
Es blitzt.	zig zag gestures in air	lightning
Und alle sind schnell	one hand and then	
ins Haus geflitzt!	the other disappears behind back	

Teach this using some large weather pictures and start with just the first two lines 'es *tropft*' and '*es regnet*'. Add the other lines bit by bit until the complete rhyme is built up. This will take several sessions and needs to be paced to suit your own children.

A well-known French rhyme with the weather as its theme is *Il pleut, il mouille*:

Use big pictures to support the words and teach phrase by phrase: '*il pleut*' and then '*il mouille*'. Split up the longer lines '*c'est la fête/à la grenouille*', etc. Always break down what is being learned into manageable pieces.

Il pleut, il mouille,

C'est la fête à la grenouille,

Il pleut, il fait beau temps.

C'est la fête au paysan

And for the winter around Christmas time you could introduce:

AAA, der Winter ist da

AAA, der Winter ist da.	everyone shivers
EEE, er bringt Eis und Schnee.	snow falling with fingers
OOO, die Kinder sind froh.	everyone dances on the spot

For Advent this little rhyme, spoken or sung, revisits those early numbers once more. This could be combined with cultural information explaining how Advent is more significant in German speaking areas with Advent wreaths of pine and four candles found in all public places including offices and shops and not just homes. You could light a candle every Monday for each of the four weeks of Advent.

Advent

Advent, Advent,
ein Lichtlein brennt.
Erst eins,   put up fingers
dann zwei,
dann drei,
dann vier.
Dann steht das Christkind vor der Tür.

Here is the notation:

PETS AND ANIMALS

Young children learn from everything around them. They love to see and touch soft cuddly toys and these are a very useful resource when we want children to listen, understand and speak. The cuddly toys can provide the bank of animal vocabulary which we want to teach, and reinforce phrases such as '*Voici . . .*', '*As-tu . . ?*', '*J'ai . . .*'/'*Hier ist . . .*' and so on.

So now we turn to some rhymes using pets and animals as the theme. The first is a finger rhyme in German.

Ein großer Hund,	index finger and little finger up
eine kleine Katze.	bend index finger and little finger
Da kommt die Maus,	other hand runs across
und das Spiel ist aus.	hands behind back

The following French rhyme is accompanied by several movements to be done by the children or by their toys.

Nounours

Nounours, nounours	teddy bear
Touche le nez	touch nose
Nounours, nounours	
Touche les pieds	touch feet
Nounours, nounours	
Saute en l'air	jump up
Nounours, nounours	
Tombe par terre	'fall down'

If we sing fresh words using familiar tunes, then the rhythm and intonation of the new words can fit into patterns already assimilated by the children. For instance, we can hold two cuddly toys and set them to music

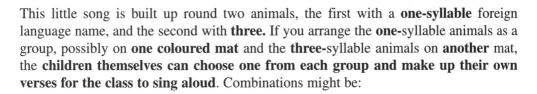

Tune: *Nuts in May*
Voici un renne et un kangourou, kangourou, kangourou
Voici un renne et un kangourou, kan-gou-rou

The children **do not even need to read the words in order to practise them in this way.** They can all focus visually on the toys held up by you or a pupil for the class to see.

This little song is built up round two animals, the first with a **one-syllable** foreign language name, and the second with **three.** If you arrange the **one-**syllable animals as a group, possibly on **one coloured mat** and the **three-**syllable animals on **another** mat, the **children themselves can choose one from each group and make up their own verses for the class to sing aloud.** Combinations might be:

Voici un chat et un crocodile	*Voici un phoque et un papillon*
Voici un chien et un éléphant	*Voici un ours et une coccinelle,* etc

In this way, the children are already at the beginning stages of being creative with the foreign language. The list is endless and only limited by the amount of cuddly toys (or pictures of animals) which are available in the classroom.

Incidentally, the above activity helps to 'educate the ear', as the children are actually 'sorting by sound'. They cannot sort the animals correctly unless they are able to 'hear' the syllables in their heads.

For very young learners this little song can become a useful, familiar routine with which to warm up or wind down at the beginning or end of a session. The same objective can be achieved in German

<table>
<tr><td>Tune:
Nuts in May</td><td>Hier ist ein Hund und ein Papagei.
Hier ist ein Fisch und ein Elefant.
Hier ist ein Bär und ein Schmetterling.
Hier ist ein Pferd und ein Krokodil.</td><td>hold the two animals up
each time</td></tr>
</table>

Clearly you will need to anticipate any alterations to the rhythm pattern which would be made by gender.

ROUNDS AND CANONS

Other tunes can be used to practise the words in different ways. As they are singing a fresh song, your children's interest will be maintained. Sometimes it is possible to use simple rounds and canons.

For example in German you might be teaching a series of animals with different genders, so you need to be saying '**ein'** *Bär* (masculine) and '**eine'** *Katze* (feminine). Naturally you will not be mentioning gender as such, but you can already train the children to hear the difference by first of all establishing the 'rhythm' of both words. Using cuddly toys or pictures, sing to the tune of *London's burning* making sure that children can hear and reproduce the correct number of syllables.

<table>
<tr><td>Tune:
London's burning</td><td>Eine Katze, eine Katze,
eine Katze, eine Katze.
Ein Bär, ein Bär,
eine Katze, eine Katze.</td></tr>
</table>

Invent similar verses, using words from each set to fit into the rhythm pattern of the song, for example:

<table>
<tr><td>Tune: London's burning</td><td>Eine Schlange, eine Schlange.
Ein Hund, ein Hund.</td></tr>
</table>

Everyone can walk around the classroom following the 'leader' who is carrying the appropriate toy and make the rhythm of the words fit their footsteps. This initial activity builds up an awareness of the 'rhythm' of the individual words. Eventually you can use the pairs you have practised **to build up to a combination**, still based on the same tune. If you have them, pick up the actual toys as they occur to support your learners' understanding.

<table>
<tr><td>Tune: London's burning</td><td>Eine Katze, eine Katze.
Eine Schlange, eine Schlange.
Ein Fisch, ein Fisch.
Ein Kaninchen, ein Kaninchen.</td></tr>
</table>

If you do not have such an array of toys, you can still support your learners by holding up pictures or photographs, or blutacking them to the board in the pairs to match the verses. Or you can 'write' the song 'visually' by producing some simple sketches on a big song card along these lines:

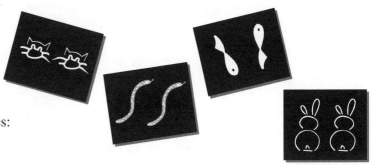

With very young learners use **pictures on their own without the words**. Here is an example of the same tune being used in French:

<table>
<tr><td>Tune:
London's burning</td><td>J'ai un poisson, j'ai un poisson
J'ai un lapin, j'ai un lapin</td><td>(J'ai) un chat, (j'ai) un chat
J'ai une souris, j'ai une souris</td></tr>
</table>

CiLT

Young Pathfinder 6: *Let's join in! Rhymes, poems and songs* — 25

Bringing it all together: fitting in with other primary themes

Finally, we round off our consideration of Key Stage 1 and Beginners with an extended example of one way in which the patterns and words from a variety of rhymes and songs can be re-worked and fitted into a topic which occurs as an annual part of the normal primary curriculum: Christmas.

A Nativity play

Start by singing the seasonal greeting *'Joyeux Noël'* to the tune of *Westminster chimes*, getting your children to mime, copy and echo in the way with which they are familiar. This activity is good to help children to practise pitch and can be done in a couple of minutes in music sessions.

Other Christmas vocabulary items can be introduced with pictures and supported by song. So you can use pictures of Father Christmas with his reindeer and sleigh and sing to *Nuts in May:* ⟶

Voici un renne et le Père Noël

You can also adapt **parts** of English carols sung regularly by children to present and practise other key figures in the Christmas story. Using pictures or realia of Mary, Joseph and the baby Jesus (see p29) add:

Tune: *Away in a manger*	*Marie et Joseph et l'enfant Jésus. Marie et Joseph et l'enfant Jésus* *Marie et Joseph et l'enfant Jésus. Marie et Joseph et l'enfant Jésus*

Ask the question *'Qui est-ce?'* and the children can reply *'Marie'*, *'Joseph'*, *'Jésus'* (NB do not use the term *'le bébé Jésus'* but either *'Jésus'*, *'le bébé'* or *'l'enfant Jésus'*). Or *'C'est le renne, c'est le Père Noël. C'est le bonhomme de neige'* whom they can greet *'Bonjour, bonhomme de neige'* or say goodbye to *'Au revoir, Père Noël'*.

In German this becomes:

Tune: *Away in a manger*	*Maria, Josef und das Jesukind. Maria, Josef und das Jesukind.* *Maria, Josef und das Jesukind. Maria, Josef und das Jesukind.*

It is **not necessary to teach or adapt whole verses**. Children tend to 'know' the op
ening lines best of all anyway and we can exploit this fact.

Another English carol you can adapt for the shepherds and their sheep goes as follows:

<table>
<tr><td>Tune: We wish you a merry Christmas</td><td>Les bergers et les moutons
Les bergers et les moutons
Les bergers et les moutons
Sont à Bethléem</td><td>Die Hirten und die Schafe,
die Hirten und die Schafe,
die Hirten und die Schafe
sind in Bethlehem.</td></tr>
</table>

Year 2 learners can even get their tongues round this adaptation of *We three Kings of Orient are*. You will need pictures or models of Jesus and the three kings (see p29), together with a star and some wrapped 'presents'.

<table>
<tr><td>Tune: We three Kings of Orient are</td><td>Les trois rois regardent l'étoile
Les trois rois regardent l'étoile
Regardez, regardez
Des cadeaux pour l'enfant Jésus</td><td>Die drei Könige sehen den Stern.
Die drei Könige sehen den Stern.
Gold, Weihrauch und Myrrhe
haben sie für das Jesukind.</td></tr>
</table>

We now suggest a way in to a very simple Nativity Play for Key Stage 1. The children can say part of the framework in English. It does not matter at all that there is a blend of English and the foreign language. They might start by announcing: 'Mary and Joseph are on their way to Bethlehem, where Mary's baby will soon be born'. Then a group can sing:

or in German

<table>
<tr><td>Tune: O little town of Bethlehem</td><td>Tune: We wish you a merry Christmas</td></tr>
</table>

A Bethléem, à Bethléem, Joseph et Marie
A Bethléem, à Bethléem, Joseph et Marie
Une chambre, une chambre, une chambre, s'il vous plaît
A Bethléem, à Bethléem, Joseph et Marie

Josef und Maria,
Josef und Maria,
Josef und Maria
sind in Bethlehem.

You will recall that in our ideas for finger rhymes, we suggested using the finger rhyme '*M. Pouce*' (p6). This example shows how a little finger rhyme already practised many times can lead naturally into re-use in a different context. Here are just the words again to remind you.

M. Pouce est dans sa maison   *C'est moi . . .*
Toc, toc, toc   *Chut. Je dors*
Qui est là?

Re-worked for the Nativity Play this becomes:

Mary and Joseph	Innkeeper
Toc, Toc, Toc	*Qui est là?*
C'est moi, Joseph]	[*Non! Non! Non!*
C'est moi, Marie]	[*Pas de chambres!*
Mais! Toc, toc, toc	*Qui est là?*
C'est moi, Joseph]	[*Voici une étable*
C'est moi, Marie]	[*Entrez.*
	[*Asseyez-vous!*

The same applies to the German rhyme *Wo ist der Daumen?* with its response *'Hier bin ich! Hier bin ich!'* The final line in the dialogue also recaps the regularly required classroom instruction *'Setz dich!'*

Mary and Joseph	Innkeeper	
Klopf! Klopf! Klopf!	*Guten Morgen!*	
Hier bin ich, Josef!]	[*Nein, Nein!*	
Hier bin ich Maria!]	[*Nein, Nein!*	
Klopf! Klopf! Klopf!	*Guten Morgen!*	
Hier bin ich Josef!]	[*Hier ist ein Stall!*	
Hier bin ich Maria!]	[*Setz dich Josef!*	pointing first to Joseph
	[*Setz dich Maria!*	then to Mary

The announcer goes on 'The innkeeper allowed Mary and Joseph to stay in his stable. That night, Mary's baby was born' and the adaptation of *Away in a manger* can be sung.

You can even re-work more of the classroom language introduced at the start of this Pathfinder for the shepherds and the angel. The announcer continues: 'Outside Bethlehem there were some shepherds looking after their sheep on the hillside. Suddenly there was a bright light. An angel/some angels appeared and spoke to them.'

The play goes on with the 'angel' appearing to the shepherds saying a little speech along the following lines. This could be said by one child or by a group as appropriate.

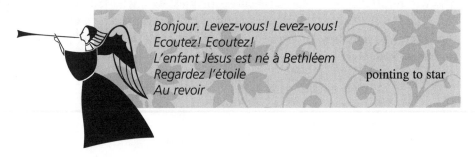

Bonjour. Levez-vous! Levez-vous!
Ecoutez! Ecoutez!
L'enfant Jésus est né à Bethléem
Regardez l'étoile   pointing to star
Au revoir

28 — Young Pathfinder 6: *Let's join in! Rhymes, poems and songs*

CiLT

Guten Abend!
Steh auf! Steh auf! — pointing to each shepherd in turn
Hör zu! Hör zu! — hands behind ear
Das Jesukind ist in Bethlehem
Sieh her! Sieh her! — pointing to star
Auf Wiedersehen!

This section is followed with a singing of '*les bergers et les moutons*' or '*die Hirten und die Schafe*' as above, after which the announcer says 'Three Kings travelled to Bethlehem from the east, with presents for the Baby Jesus. They looked at the star, which led them to the stable.' The play is rounded off with a rendition of *Les trois rois/die drei Könige* to the tune of *We three Kings of Orient are*.

So you can see that everything fits in perfectly, even though in Key Stage 1 nothing has required the children to recognise letters or text. Although many activities with beginners concentrate on introducing and practising **individual words**, by means of simple structures and straightforward finger and action rhymes and songs, children have progressed to **repeating sentences** in a fun way. Indeed, when they sing rhymes, whether your own or traditional ones, they are also developing the ability to repeat the foreign language fluently at speed, since they are keeping up with the tune and the music and rhythm are carrying them forward. These combine to form a stress free taster experience of foreign language work, while simultaneously developing oral skills and the ability to listen attentively, both to their teachers and to each other, as in the simple performances and drama activities suggested above.

Les bergers et les moutons
Die Hirten und die Schafe

Jésus, Marie et l'enfant Jésus
Josef, Maria und das Jesukind

Les trois rois
Die Drei Könige

PART 2
Moving on: Key Stage 2 and beyond

In Key Stage 2, when learners' literacy and numeracy skills in their mother tongue are more developed, we continue to adopt similar strategies involving actions and movement but we can also draw on the children's growing reading and writing skills. The latter not only help children in their learning **of** the foreign language, but can themselves be developed and enriched **by** the learning of the foreign language.

The same topics mentioned in Part 1 are revisited, and many of the strategies suggested for beginning learners will be appropriate in Key Stages 2 and 3. However, it is essential, particularly for children in Years 5 and 6 and above, to recycle previously taught language in new ways, so that they are aware of working differently from either younger pupils or foreign language learners at an earlier stage. If the children themselves are not aware of this sense of moving forward, many will feel disheartened at what they see as repeating either the same work as they have done before, or as younger pupils in their school are doing.

 ### LET'S JOIN IN: RHYMES TO SAY WITH A PHYSICAL RESPONSE

As in Part 1, we start with spoken rhymes which do not require a cassette recorder or musical instruments. The examples which follow keep each of the children busy doing the actions.

GREETINGS

We return to the **greetings** theme with a rhyme in German which can be chanted rhythmically and accompanied by simple actions. Children stand up and shake hands with other pupils round their table.

Hände schütteln	
Hände schütteln, Hände schütteln,	shake hands with person to right
ist ein schöner Brauch.	
Hände schütteln, Hände schütteln,	shake hands with person to left
geht in England auch!	

If you have more space, this can be done in a circle too, with children dancing round the circle giving each other their hands in an English 'chain' as they move from partner to partner.

LOOK AT ME!

A finger rhyme which can be recited by children sitting in their places and which is short but with more unusual vocabulary than we introduced in Part 1 is the following:

> **Beau front**
> *Beau front*   touch your forehead
> *Beaux yeux*   touch your eyes
> *Nez de cancan*   touch your nose
> *Bouche d'argent*   touch your mouth
> *Menton fleuri*   touch your chin
> *Guili-guili-guili*   tickle yourself

This brings us to some more rhymes incorporating larger body movements. In Part 1, we introduced the short and simple action rhyme *Mes petites mains font tap! Tap! Tap!* which mentioned hands and feet only. The following rhyme continues and extends the theme, adding in arms and the whole body. You will note that it ends with a movement which brings the children quietly back into their seats!

Mes petits pieds

Mes petits pieds font tap! Tap! Tap!	tap feet
Mes petites mains font clap! Clap! Clap!	clap hands
Mes petits bras sont en l'air	put hands up in air
Mes petits pieds sautent par terre	jump up and down
Nos petits corps tournent en rond	turn round
Et s'asseyent gentiment	sit down quietly

PUTTING THINGS IN THE RIGHT ORDER: SEQUENCING

One skill which young learners have to develop is the ability to put things in the correct order, for example a sequence of numbers, letters of the alphabet, days of the week, months of the year, the seasons . . . So we now return to the popular topic of counting in the foreign language. You will remember that the counting activities in Part 1 all involved counting forwards, so here is an action rhyme for counting to ten in German.

COUNTING FORWARDS

You will notice that is has **extremely short lines**, based on individual words (the numbers one to ten in this case) single nouns (*Polizei, Offizier, alte Hex*) and just two greetings (*'Gute Nacht'* and *'Auf Wiedersehen'*). It has a strong rhythmical beat which helps the sequence of numbers stick in the learner's memory.

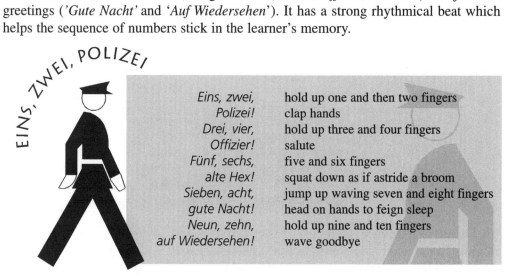

Eins, zwei,	hold up one and then two fingers
Polizei!	clap hands
Drei, vier,	hold up three and four fingers
Offizier!	salute
Fünf, sechs,	five and six fingers
alte Hex!	squat down as if astride a broom
Sieben, acht,	jump up waving seven and eight fingers
gute Nacht!	head on hands to feign sleep
Neun, zehn,	hold up nine and ten fingers
auf Wiedersehen!	wave goodbye

COUNTING BACKWARDS

Counting forwards is a good beginning and shows the ability to memorise a sound sequence. In contrast, the following rhymes get the children to **count backwards** which is an appropriate next step. Children will be familiar with these kinds of pattern from rhymes such as *There were ten in the bed* which 'take one away'. (Any changes to the pattern of the words is highlighted.)

Six au lit
Et le petit dit
'Poussez vous! Poussez-vous!'

5, 4, 3

Deux *au lit*
Et le petit dit
'Pousse-toi! Pousse-toi!'

Plus personne au lit
Et le petit dit
'Bonne nuit'

The number of children to fit the rhyme can stand in a row. Everyone says the rhyme and at the end of each line, one pupil sits down on *'Poussez-vous'*. The last child makes a sleepy gesture. Learners in Key Stage 2 are often still receptive to the use of toys in the classroom. A variation might include illustrating the song by removing one toy each time one is pushed 'out of bed'.

32 — Young Pathfinder 6: *Let's join in! Rhymes, poems and songs*

CiLT

Here is a German equivalent:

Es gab zehn im Bett,
und der kleinste sagte:
'Rutscht 'rüber, rutscht 'rüber!'
Sie rutschten alle rüber,
und einer fiel heraus . . .

Es gab **neun** im Bett,
und der kleinste sagte:
'Rutscht 'rüber, rutscht 'rüber!'
Sie rutschten alle rüber,
und einer fiel heraus.

Es gab 8, 7, 6, 5, 4, 3, 2 . . .

Es gab **einen** im Bett,
und der kleinste sagte:
'Gute Nacht! Gute Nacht!'

Of course, **you do not have to begin back at ten**, you could start as in the French example, at six, or even three, four, or five or whatever suits your learners. The important thing is that, with the exception of the final verse, **the children have only one change to make**, and that is the number, with **which they are already familiar**.

The following rhyme is more challenging still, because the fingers are also changed with a corresponding new word in each verse. However, if the pupils have been learning some of the shorter finger rhymes suggested in Part 1, they will be recycling the various names for the different fingers.

Fünf kleine Fingerlein tanzen herum.	all five fingers in air wiggle them	Zwei kleine Fingerlein tanzen herum.	two fingers
Der Daumen, der mag nicht mehr.	hide one thumb	Der Ringfinger, der mag nicht mehr.	hide fourth finger
Ach wie dumm!		Ach wie dumm!	
Vier kleine Fingerlein tanzen herum.	four fingers	Ein kleines Fingerlein tanzt herum.	little finger
Der Zeigefinger, der mag nicht mehr.	hide forefinger!	Der kleine Finger, der mag nicht mehr.	hide little finger
Ach wie dumm!		Ach wie dumm!	
Drei kleine Fingerlein tanzen herum.	three fingers		
Der Mittelfinger, der mag nicht mehr.	hide middle finger		
Ach wie dumm!			

Fünf kleine Fingerlein

As the children learn to manipulate numbers in this way, they will begin to have a better developed sense of numeracy in the foreign language.

DAYS OF THE WEEK

Another topic which involves remembering in the right order is the 'days of the week'. To prepare for the rhyme make flashcards either with a picture/symbol for each day of the week, or simply with the beginning letter(s) (*L for 'lundi', Ma- for Mardi, Me- for Mercredi,* etc). Alternatively, you can simply write the day of the week cues out in clear lower case letters.

As a first step, present the days of the week holding up the cues, one by one, with the children echoing each word. As the days are recited aloud, place the visuals in the correct order, so that children are finally reading aloud along the whole sequence from left to right. This technique establishes a sequence of sounds in the mind of the learner, and learning is reinforced by the written word on the flashcards, which provide the sequence in visual form.

In a subsequent session, place the flashcards in the correct order, face up. You can prop the cards up along the ledge of the board if you have one. Run through the sequence altogether. Then turn one card over, and get everyone to recite the sequence including the one which is no longer visible. Gradually increase the number of face down cards until all are reversed and the whole sequence is being said from memory.

As a third stage, start where you left off before, and attach the correct sequence to the board, get children to close their eyes and **remove one or two cards.** Children open their eyes and have to 'read' inside their heads to identify the one or two that have been removed.

A fourth stage can also start with the word cards in the correct sequence, face up. While children have their eyes closed **swap two days over**. Now the children have to identify the ones which have been 'misplaced' **and help replace them in the correct sequence**.

You can give a row of seven pupils a 'weekday' flashcard each to hold, which they show as the following rhyme is recited. They can either simply hold them up or they can have the cue face towards them and turn the flashcard over as the day is spoken. You could adopt similar strategies when learning **the months.**

*Bonjour Madame **Lundi***	turn over/show Monday flashcard
*Comment va Madame **Mardi**?*	show Tuesday flashcard
*Très bien Madame **Mercredi***	show Wednesday flashcard
*Dites à Madame **Jeudi***	show Thursday flashcard
*De venir **vendredi***	show Friday flashcard
*Danser **samedi***	show Saturday flashcard
*Dans la salle de **dimanche**!*	show Sunday flashcard

PREPARING FOR READING AND WRITING

THE FOREIGN LANGUAGE ALPHABET

When learners are really secure with the pronunciation and sequence of the alphabet in English, the foreign language alphabet can be practised alongside. Covering skills in a foreign language often gives pupils a second chance to learn them. Practising spelling in the foreign language helps not only with the development of literacy in the foreign language, but with the development of spelling in general.

You do not need to start by teaching the whole alphabet at all. Simply begin by spelling out key words such as B-O-N-J-O-U-R, S-A-L-U-T or G-U-T-E-N T-A-G. The important thing is to **build up gradually from very small beginnings.** Draw up individual letters on small flashcards (or use peel-off letter stickers) and blutack a selection to the board in the order in which the word is spelt. Chorus the spelling aloud together.

You can then randomly stick the letters which make up these familiar words to the board in a jumbled way and get pupils to look at them for a moment. Say each letter aloud together. Tell pupils to shut their eyes *'Fermez les yeux/Augen zu'*. While they are doing so, remove one or several letter cards. At the command *'Ouvrez les yeux/Augen auf'* children open their eyes and you ask *'Qu'est-ce qui manque?/Was fehlt?'* Pupils tell you which letter(s) has (have) gone, and you show them the missing letter(s) to confirm, pronouncing the letter names in the foreign language once more.

When you have introduced most letters, one way of practising the alphabet (or other language items) is to do **clapping sequences** based on playground games. Here is an example. Children stand up opposite a partner.

A B C	clap own hands	x 3
D E F	clap to partner	x 3
G H I J K	clap knees	x 5
L M N	clap own hands	x 3
O P Q	clap partner's hands right	x 3
R S T	clap partner's hands left	x 3
U V W X Y	alternate hands one at a time	*C'est l'alphabet français*
Z	large overhead clap with partner	*Das ist das deutsche Alphabet*

You can reinforce the alphabet by chanting other spellings. Every day choose three or four words and spell them aloud for the children to guess. If these words are the names of children in the class, this gives the learners a clearly defined topic area within which to guess, e.g. H-A-N-N-A-H. If you wish you can write out large lower case name cards for each member of the class and everyone can practise spelling with the support of the visual prompt. This also helps letter shape recognition. When the children are very comfortable themselves with using the foreign language alphabet actively, they can take over the teacher's role.

The next step is to actively focus on how individual words other than proper nouns are spelled. You can do this by writing up a well-known word such as *'Bonjour'* and spell it out loud together as above. Then get the children to close their eyes while you rub out firstly just one of the letters. Children tell you which letter is missing when they open their eyes. This can be developed by rubbing out progressively more letters, two and then three at random. With practice many children will be able to spell complete words in the foreign language from memory. Ask *'Bonjour. Ça s'écrit comment?'*

When children already know the alphabet including the vowels in their mother tongue, this poem *Voyelles* by Arthur Rimbaud is easily learned and will help reinforce this knowledge. It can be 'read' aloud from a text written in the appropriate colours, working along similar principles as described in Part 1.

Voyelles	Visual text
A noir	A (written in black)
E blanc	E (written in white on dark background)
I rouge	I (written in red)
O bleu	O (written in blue)
U vert	U (written in green)
Voyelles!	*Voyelles!*

In French it will be helpful to be able to identify the vowels later on when the pupils are being taught rules such as the use of the apostrophe in words such as *'l'arbre'* which affect both spelling and pronunciation.

Perhaps when you are revisiting the alphabet and spellings you might like children to learn this rhyme.

A B C D E	*Der Kopf tut mir weh*
F G H I J K	*Der Doktor ist da*
L M N O	*Jetzt bin ich froh*
P Q R S T	*Es ist gut, juchhe!*
U V W X	*Jetzt fehlt mir nix*
Y Z	*Jetzt geh ich ins Bett*

Pupils can mount a display featuring their own illustrated alphabet frieze. Each child can take responsibility for contributing a letter. You could sing one of the many commercially available alphabet songs (see Appendix) which practise the sequence A–Z and children could talk about the alternative versions.

36 — Young Pathfinder 6: *Let's join in! Rhymes, poems and songs*

CiLT

RECOGNISING PATTERNS

This kind of regular work on developing children's knowledge of alphabetical and numerical order contributes to the building blocks of literacy and numeracy. The ability to recognise and reproduce a pattern is an important skill, which contributes to all language learning in general. The pattern can be a sound pattern, or a visual one such as colours, shapes or words.

Words have patterns of letters within them, words build into phrases and sentences, phrases and sentences build into blocks of text or chunks of language. We help the young learner to internalise the patterns which exist in language using many multisensory ways — rhythm, sound, visual, movement.

CIRCLE TIME

During circle time the children can create patterns in the foreign language with a few words and build up to ever longer phrases.

Why not try creating a Mexican wave *(La Holà)*. Use the playground, assembly hall, or carpet area in your classroom, anywhere with enough space for the children to sit in a circle. Explain in English that something is going to 'travel' round the circle. Do an example in English to familiarise the children with circle activity, for instance, everyone says their own name in turn. At the same time as they say their name, they stand up, and sit down when the names are travelling back round again. Add further interest by changing the travelling direction at a certain signal for instance, when you clap, children must change direction and send the words back again.

In the foreign language, the first stage can be saying **one** well-known word only, e.g. *'Bonjour'*. As in the practice example, add visual interest as before by getting children to stand up when it is their turn to say *'Bonjour'* and sit down when repeating it.

Build up by using **two or three words**, perhaps numbers or letters of the alphabet, counting 1-2-3, 1-2-3 or saying A, B, C, A, B, C, around the circle. When you have taught a series of numbers, children can count up to 30 in one direction, standing up on their number, then down from 30, sitting down on their number. You can even incorporate the expressions from finger rhymes taught in Key Stage 1 as follows:

Toc, toc, toc	three children knock on heads one after the other
Qui est là?	next child opens hand in gesture
Toc, toc, toc	three children knock on heads one after the other
Qui est là?	next child opens hands in questioning gesture
	and so on round the circle

Finally, whole poems can be rehearsed in this way. For instance, the first step for *Eins, zwei Polizei* can be just those three words which travel round the circle in groups of three *'Eins, zwei, Polizei, eins zwei, Polizei, eins, zwei, Polizei.'* On another occasion, add in the next two lines *'Drei, vier, Offizier'* with the gestures and build up to the complete poem round the circle.

ORIENTATION ON A PAGE OF TEXT

Children benefit not only by learning spelling patterns in the foreign language, but also by looking at blocks of text on a page so that they develop the skill of locating themselves when looking for cues when reading. Here is an action rhyme which helps with **orientation on a page of text and/or visuals:**

En haut de la page	point to ceiling
En bas de la page	point to floor
Au milieu de la page	point straight ahead
A droite de la page	point to right
A gauche de la page	point to left
Au milieu de la page	point straight ahead

This skill of orientation can be practised by playing a game using flashcards of well-known vocabulary to encourage the children do place them orally on the page. Draw up a 'noughts and crosses' grid on the board, and place nine flashcards in the boxes. For example:

4 = *en haut de la page, à gauche*
3 = *en haut de la page, au milieu*
8 = *en haut de la page, à droite*
2 = *au milieu de la page, à gauche*
5 = *au milieu de la page*
1 = *au milieu de la page, à droite*
9 = *en bas de la page, à gauche*
7 = *en bas de la page, au milieu*
6 = *en bas de la page, à droite*

4	3	8
2	5	1
9	7	6

In the illustration we have used numbers. Start with a simple touching activity. Ask the children *'Touchez en haut de la page'*. In response, children can place their hands across the top line. Go on to practise *'Touchez au milieu de la page'* and *'Touchez en bas de la page'*.

Progress to being more precise: *'Touchez en haut de la page **à gauche**'*, etc. In this activity children are simply showing that they understand.

As a next step, ask the children to tell you which number or flashcard fits in which box: *'Au milieu de la page, c'est quel numéro?'* Response: *'5'*.

Finally, **turn the question round:** '*Le numéro 5, c'est où?*' The children tell you where on the grid the number fits, so the answer this time becomes '*Au milieu de la page*'.

This game can be played with letters of the alphabet, pictures of well-known vocabulary and words of rhymes and songs, when the children are able to read text. Discuss reading conventions at the same time in English, reminding children of the way the eye travels from left to right and from top to bottom on the page.

 ## LINKING THE SPOKEN WORD WITH ITS WRITTEN FORM

With very young learners or beginners we have shown how songs and rhymes can support the development of literacy and numeracy skills and yet be taught **without using print** by means of a variety of visual stimuli as prompts for the spoken word:

- **actions**
- **realia**
- **classroom objects**
- **visuals**

which all help illustrate the meaning and act as concrete representations for the sounds the children were hearing or saying. It is important that children see the **written word as a natural extension** of this, and not as a difficult or problematic element of their language learning.

So now we suggest another dimension, the use of text both in the foreign language and in the mother tongue. Although this technique is **not recommended** in Key Stage 1, once basic literacy skills have been established during Key Stage 2, reading in the foreign language can start to be developed as a skill and rhymes, poems and songs can be shown to pupils as written texts to be read or sung aloud.

It is **not** advisable to ask learners in the early stages to read written material which has not been produced orally. Working out how the words are to be pronounced and attempting to reproduce them is threatening and often leads to disaster. Far better to wait until the written word acts as a reinforcement to prior oral/aural learning. It is particularly important when working with French to delay the introduction of the written form until the spoken form is quite secure, as the spelling and pronunciation cause problems if introduced too soon.

One way in is for Key Stage 2 pupils to start by reading, illustrating and eventually, copywriting rhymes and songs learnt orally in Key Stage 1 without written words. It is vital that the **reading be developed in harmony with speaking and listening skills and not in isolation**. In this way, there is a natural progression in skills development between Key Stages 1 and 2 and it is possible to re-visit some of the same language material and yet exploit it in a different way.

A SIMPLE EXAMPLE — COUNTING

Here is a well-known traditional **counting rhyme**, limited to the numbers one to twelve, which shows how you can combine both text plus the appropriate illustrations to begin to introduce word recognition in the foreign language. It uses the minimum of written words (the numbers) which have been taught orally first.

Un, deux, trois
Nous irons aux bois
Quatre, cinq, six
Cueillir des cerises
Sept huit neuf
Dans mon panier neuf
Dix onze douze
Elles seront toutes rouges

Don't forget to say the words aloud with lots of rhythm and emphasis, even when the written or printed word is being introduced.

This authentic poem by Claude Roy builds on the numbers already taught — you can ask the children to spot the number which is missing!

40 — Young Pathfinder 6: *Let's join in! Rhymes, poems and songs*

CiLT

A MORE COMPLICATED EXAMPLE — COLOURS

Colours can be reinforced in a very simple text based round a few nouns and the colours. Begin by teaching or revising the colours, using colour cards or objects in the colours you require. You will need items to represent the colours green, blue, yellow, grey, brown, red, black and white. Then present the nouns in the poem separately on flashcards using pictures which are already coloured in to match the colours in the poem. Do not draw attention to the colours to begin with. Use visuals for grass, the sky, sand, a mouse, a bear, a rose, a piece of coal and some bread. After having practised the colours *'Das ist grün. Wie ist das? Das ist grün',* etc. and the objects *'Das Gras. Was ist das? Das Gras'* you can combine the two in simple sentences. *'Das Gras ist grün. Der Bär ist braun.'*

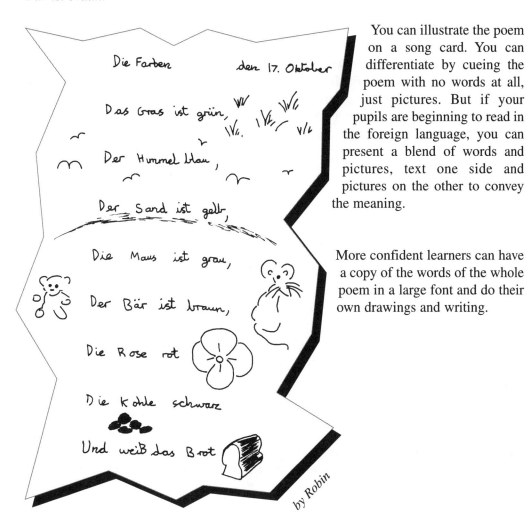

Die Farben   den 17. Oktober

Das Gras ist grün,

Der Himmel blau,

Der Sand ist gelb,

Die Maus ist grau,

Der Bär ist braun,

Die Rose rot

Die Kohle schwarz

Und weiß das Brot

by Robin

You can illustrate the poem on a song card. You can differentiate by cueing the poem with no words at all, just pictures. But if your pupils are beginning to read in the foreign language, you can present a blend of words and pictures, text one side and pictures on the other to convey the meaning.

More confident learners can have a copy of the words of the whole poem in a large font and do their own drawings and writing.

Let's read together

One way in to written texts such as the poem above is to arouse children's interest by reciting a favourite English nursery rhyme or poem to the class and asking children to tell you if they know it too. They will probably have plenty of their own examples to share. Highlight the rhyming words and discuss why rhymes are easy to remember: you might talk about strong rhythms, actions, tunes, the fun element, frequency, rhyme and repetition. Then show a poster-size version of a very short foreign language rhyme to read and learn together. For example, if you want to recycle rhymes from Key Stage 1 with older children, you can introduce them at this point in their written form. Even when you are presenting more text, make sure there are at least some pictures to support the words.

WEATHER AND SEASONS

Short poems which feature the weather, seasons and festivals are especially appropriate for this purpose. You can **add further verses** (where there are any) to rhymes you already know, to add variety and give a sense of progress. Most can be accompanied by simple sketches to help learners internalise the meaning of the text. Alternative verses to *il pleut, il mouille* are:

Il pleut, il mouille	Il pleut, il mouille
C'est la fête à la grenouille	C'est la fête à la grenouille
Il pleut, il fait beau temps	Quand il ne pleuvra plus
C'est la fête au cerf-volant	Ça sera la fête à la tortue

As a progression from the colours and seasons which children have already learned, the following traditional little poem could form part of a harvest assembly, and be illustrated with pictures as suggested elsewhere. Before you present any rhyme or poem look at the text carefully to see if there are nouns or expressions which you can pre-teach, in this case 'yellow and red leaves', a calendar picture for autumn and summer, a rainy scene. Teach these items separately first. Then show the written equivalents on word flashcards. Read aloud together and carry out some **matching tasks**, with children putting word and caption cards on the visual cues. By matching words and pictures in this way the spoken word is connected to its printed or written form. Then introduce the whole poem.

ciLT

Automne

Il pleut
Des feuilles jaunes
Il pleut
Des feuilles rouges
L'été
Va s'endormir

Et l'hiver
Va venir
Sur la pointe
De ses souliers
Gelés

Anne Marie Chapouton

Rhymes and song texts can be **read aloud together** from an illustrated OHP. At this stage, it is helpful to have the written form of the song supported by visuals and/or accompanying actions so that the meaning is always transparently clear.

Show a large written version on an OHP or chart. Reveal words one at a time, or in small 'sense' groups and encourage your pupils to read along with you. Try reciting some of the words in an exaggerated way, read loudly and emphatically, and then very quietly indeed. Reading aloud together in chorus is a valuable midway stage between simply listening, and speaking out on one's own. Because everyone is following the same sequence, your learners are supporting each other. There is the added security of knowing that everyone else is following and reciting the same text, and of 'knowing what comes next', whereas in much interactive pair work the learner is faced with the spontaneous and unpredictable.

As a variation, you can produce a jumbo sized rhyme book with words large enough to be visible to the whole class for reading from altogether. It is important when reading aloud together to do so with expression and to keep up a reasonable pace. Class teachers will be familiar with the use of large story books for reading during literacy hour, which involve the whole class in choral reading a story with expression and meaning. The same techniques can be used when reading the text of a rhyme or song instead of a story, building children's confidence in themselves as readers.

 LET'S WRITE

Some more rhymes on a rainy theme in German follow. At this stage you could ask pupils to design something visual to help them remember the words and phrases. The following rhyme might form the basis for two captions beneath two weather pictures, one with the rain and the other depicting a fine day. Reading and writing must be introduced in graduated steps to develop oracy and literacy, so start by suggesting that pupils copy single key words and label pictures.

Es regnet

Es regnet, es regnet,   caption for picture 1
und regnet seinen Lauf!
Und wenn's genug geregnet hat, caption for picture 2
so hört es wieder auf!

April

April, April, April,
der macht, was er will!
Mal Regen und mal
Sonnenschein,
dann schneit es wieder
zwischendrein,
dann bläst der Sturmwind
kräftig drein!
April, April, April,
der macht, was er will!

Willi Regenwurm

Ich heiße Willi Regenwurm.
Ich liebe Regen und den Sturm.
In nasser Erde — oh Entzücken
wälz ich den Bauch und den Rücken!

In the Spring you may like to write the next little poem beneath pictures or a vase of catkins. Speak the lines, and get pupils to repeat after you, line by line. Recognition of the written word becomes both a tool for learning the language and also a skill which is developed as a result of learning the language.

Das Palmkätzchen

Weiches, graues Pelzchen
hat mein kleines Kätzchen.
Sitzt im braunen Häuschen
wie ein kleines Mäuschen.

FESTIVALS

Now pupils are progressing to speaking, reading and perhaps copying short phrases and sentences. At Easter either of the two following poems in German incorporate both colours and numbers and remind children of the custom of the Easter bunny.

Wer sitzt da im grünen Gras?

Wer sitzt da im grünen Gras,
mit bunten Farben, wer ist denn das?
Er malt die Eier, blau, gelb und rot
fürs Frühstück und fürs Abendbrot.
Hat eine runde Knubbelnase.
Ich glaub, das ist der Osterhase!

Das Osternest

Im Osternest, da liegt ein Ei.
Oder sind es etwa zwei?
Ein Ei ist rot,
ein Ei ist blau.
Daneben sitzt die Hasenfrau!

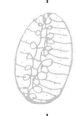

44 — Young Pathfinder 6: *Let's join in! Rhymes, poems and songs*

CILT

Here is another weather poem for winter time. Some children could paint a snowy picture while others might like to key the text in using one of the word processing packages available for schools. Children with limited writing stamina could key in one line each which would involve them in relatively short typing tasks.

> *Du liebe Zeit!*
> *Es schneit, es schneit!*
> *Die Flocken fliegen*
> *und bleiben liegen!*
> *Ach bitte sehr,*
> *noch mehr, noch mehr!*

Long sequences for copywriting are not suitable, but you can develop purposeful accurate copywriting skills by offering short foreign language verses or poems. This makes a change from simply noting down transactional language as well as introducing some cultural awareness when the poems and rhymes are traditional.

The following rhymes fit nicely inside a greetings card. You can write the words on prepared photocopies for the children to stick into their cards and illustrate. Older children can copywrite their own poem inside a Christmas card.

Tell children that 6 December is widely celebrated in Germany and Austria and that to remind themselves of Sankt Nikolaus people give each other small gifts and sweets, especially ones they have made themselves.

Petit Papa Noël
Quand tu descendras du ciel
Avec des jouets par milliers
N'oublie pas mon petit soulier!

Lieber guter Nikolas

Lieber guter Nikolas
bring den kleinen Kindern was!
Laß die großen laufen,
sie können sich was kaufen!

ANIMALS

When your class is learning about **pets and animals** you might like to incorporate some of the following traditional rhymes. The first is a finger rhyme. Again the phrase '*et puis s'en va*' and the accompanying movement is similar to what has already been met.

Une poule sur un mur

Une poule sur un mur	'peck' back of hand with index finger
Qui picotait du pain dur	of other hand
Picoti picota	peck with other index finger (swap hands)
Lève la queue et puis s'en va	hands disappear behind

At Easter time, another rhyme about three hens could be taught, with the children walking around in groups of three to emphasise the positions of first, second and third.

TROIS POULES

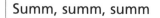

**Quand trois poules vont aux champs
La première va devant
La deuxième suit la première
La troisième va en arrière
Quand trois poules vont aux champs
La première va devant!**

In fact, there are a whole host of short poems which have animals and insects as their focus and can be learned alongside a number of primary class themes. These foreign language rhymes can be compared and contrasted with English poems which fall into similar categories. Both the French rhyme about the little fish and the German poem about the bee are based round a core of key words '*petit poisson*' and '*summ, summ, summ, Bienchen summ herum*' which are repeated and make the language less complex than it might at first appear. They also give rise to discussion about alliteration and can be compared with English versions of rhymes and poems.

Petit poisson qui tourne en rond

*Petit poisson qui tourne en rond
Petit poisson dis-moi ton nom
Petit poisson qui bouge
Petit poisson tout rouge
Petit poisson dis-moi ton nom*

Summ, summ, summ

*Summ, summ, summ,
Bienchen summ herum!
Ei, wir tun dir nichts zuleide,
flieg nur aus in Wald und Heide!
Summ, summ, summ,
Bienchen summ herum!*

Rhymes such as these can also be shown on OHP with the English text parallel, so that the meaning is presented in word form rather than entirely through visuals and realia. If you simply show the English alongside, but without making specific mention of it, this avoids the need to translate or explain using spoken English, so that all speaking can remain in the target language. Children will naturally look across to the English if they need to, and ignore it if they do not. In this way, you are acknowledging the fact that children can read in English which becomes a support. If you do not want to draw attention to the English at any point, cover it up.

Either of the next two rhymes could accompany the popular story *The hungry caterpillar* by Eric Carle.

Die Raupe
Seht die Raupe kriecht daher
auf dem Ast, das ist sehr schwer!
Seht die Raupe, frißt und frißt
bis ganz dick die Raupe ist!

Der Schmetterling
Ein kleiner Schmi-schma-Schmetterling,
der fliegt von Ort zu Ort.
Der Schmi, der Schma, der Schmetterling
ist mal da, mal dort.

The next two donkey poems would fit into a farmyard theme or could be learned near Palm Sunday.

Mon âne

Mon âne, mon âne
A bien mal à la tête
Madame lui fit faire
Un bonnet pour sa fête
Et des souliers lilas, la, la
Et des souliers lilas

Das Eselchen

Ein kleines graues Eselchen,
das trampelt durch die Welt.
Es wackelt mit dem Hinterteil,
gleich wie es ihm gefällt.
I-A, I-A, I-A, I-A, I-A

LET'S SING!

We now turn to songs. We start with a rhyme with a simple 'tune' which could be sung during a music session. Using the sol-fa scale, use hands to 'climb the ladder' of the musical scale when you sing the first part of each line. The second half of each line, which has a mime, is to the tune of the first half.

Do ré mi

Do ré mi	
La perdrix	hands flap on spot to imitate bird
Mi fa sol	
Elle s'envole	hands 'fly' up into the air
Fa mi ré	
Dans un pré	mark out shape of meadow with hands
Mi ré do	
Tombe dans l'eau	hands 'dive' into water

CREATING CONFIDENCE BY USING FAMILIAR TUNES

As we have said before, it helps learners if they are already familiar with the tune. So, for example, they may know the 'rainbow' song from English and therefore find the French version with a similar tune easy to tackle. The song has some inbuilt repetition of '*Je connais les couleurs, toutes les couleurs, de mon arc en ciel*' which means there is a limited amount to learn.

Rouge et orange et jaune et bleu
Violet, rose et vert
Je connais les couleurs
Toutes les couleurs
De mon arc en ciel.
Regarde avec les yeux

Et chante avec la voix,
Chante une chanson gaie
Je connais les couleurs
Toutes les couleurs
De mon arc en ciel français

Similarly, *Jingle bells* forms the musical basis for the French carol *Vive le vent*. Focus to begin with on the opening phrases'*Vive le vent, vive le vent d'hiver*' which occur at the start of each verse. If you have a version to listen to on cassette, your class can join in with these lines which act like a refrain and just listen to the closing two lines. When children are familiar with the *vive le vent* lines, teach the two lines which complete each verse. Talk about the sounds produced by words like '*sifflant*' '*soufflant*' and how they match the wind.

Vive le vent

Vive le vent
Vive le vent
Vive le vent d'hiver
Qui s'en va sifflant soufflant
Dans les grands sapins verts

Vive le vent
Vive le vent
Vive le vent d'hiver
Boules de neige et jour de l'an
Et bonne année grand'mère!

CiLT

CREATING CONFIDENCE BY USING FAMILIAR WORDS

Apart from using tunes which are well known, alternatively children find familiar words a help. So for example you may have been practising question and answer sequences involving birthdays and can then introduce this song on cassette.

> *Quelle est la date de ton anniversaire?*
> *Janvier février mars x 2*
> *Quelle est la date de ton anniversaire?*
> *Avril, mai, juin x 2*
> *Janvier février mars avril mai juin*
> *Juillet août septembre octobre novembre décembre*
> *Quelle est la date de ton anniversaire?*
> *Juillet août septembre x 2*
> *Quelle est la date de ton anniversaire?*
> *Octobre novembre décembre x 2*
> *Ça y est (after second singing)*

ROUNDS — COMPARING AND CONTRASTING ALTERNATIVE VERSIONS

Le coucou

Dans la forêt lointaine
On entend le coucou
Du haut de son grand chêne
Il répond au hibou
A Coucou coucou
Coucou coucou

Other well-known tunes can work very well as rounds, for example, any versions of *Frère Jacques/ Bruder Jakob* can be sung as a round in either two or four parts. Here is another song which can be sung as a two-part round by older children. At letter A (the start of the *coucou* section) the second group of children sing the song from the beginning. It is not necessary to translate. In fact, some authentic songs are a good vehicle for helping children grasp the fact that they do not have to understand every word.

The English version of *Le coucou* can be taught and sung alongside, so that children become aware that similar songs exist in their own language as well as in the foreign language.

 ## LET'S MOVE! SONGS WITH ACTIONS

A number of action songs about body parts have similar tunes in English and in the foreign language. For instance, here are foreign language versions of *Heads and shoulders, knees and toes*.

Note that the tune is already known from English, making it easier for pupils to memorise the French or German versions together with the foreign language body parts; it is very repetitive with different parts of the body eliminated each time the song is sung; it has short lines consisting of individual words.

Tête, épaules, genoux, pieds
Tête, épaules, genoux, pieds
Tête, épaules, genoux, pieds
Genoux, pieds
Yeux, oreilles
Et bouche et nez
Tête, épaules, genoux, pieds
Genoux, pieds
  * *épaules, genoux, pieds,*
  * *épaules, genoux, pieds*
Genoux, pieds
Yeux, oreilles
Bouche et nez
  * *épaules, genoux, pieds*
Genoux, pieds, etc

And in German

Kopf und Schultern, Knie und Zehen
Kopf und Schultern, Knie und Zehen,
Knie und Zehen.
Kopf und Schultern, Knie und Zehen,
Knie und Zehen.
Augen, Ohren, Mund und Nas'.
Kopf und Schultern, Knie und Zehen,
Knie und Zehen.

Missing out words and replacing them with actions, more and more in successive verses, as in the above songs, is quite complicated for younger learners, as they have to carry the words and the beat inside their heads. You can easily tell as you are watching which pupils can and which cannot yet carry the song in their heads, when you see whether they join in, do not join in or even never stop singing in the supposedly silent parts!

As an alternative you can choose a song such as *Alouette* with a refrain which children learn very quickly. It also has the advantage of verses which build up cumulatively so that those children who have not mastered it straightaway, have an added opportunity of getting the words on each successive singing.

50 — Young Pathfinder 6: *Let's join in! Rhymes, poems and songs*

CiLT

Alouette

Alouette, gentille alouette
Alouette, je te plumerai
Je te plumerai la tête
Je te plumerai la tête
Et la tête
Et la tête
Alouette
Alouette
Aaaah . . .

Refrain:
Alouette, gentille alouette
Alouette je te plumerai
Je te plumerai le bec
Je te plumerai le bec
Et le bec, etc
le dos
le ventre
les ailes
les pattes, etc

And of course the *Hokey Cokey* is a tremendously popular song with children of all ages, it is so noisy and action filled! In French this becomes:

Le gouzi-gouzi

Je mets la main devant!
Je mets la main derrière!
Je mets la main devant
Et je fais un petit rond

put hand in
put hand out
put hand in
turn round on spot!

Je fais le gouzi gouzi
Et je saute trois fois!
Un . . . deux . . . trois . . .
Et un pas sur le côté

do the hokey cokey
jump three times
1 . . . 2 . . . 3 . . .
and a side step

Oh, le gouzi-gouzi
Oh, le gouzi-gouzi
Oh, le gouzi-gouzi
Pliez les genoux et
Un . . . deux . . . trois

bend knees

Je mets le pied devant
Je mets le pied derrière
Je mets le pied devant!
Et je fais un petit rond!

put foot in

Je fais le gouzi-gouzi
Et je saute quatre fois
Un . . . deux . . . trois . . . quat'
Et un pas sur le côté

Oh, le gouzi-gouzi, etc

Continue to add in
other body parts:
la tête, le bras,
la jambe, etc

and in German:

> *Die rechte Hand 'rein,*   right hand in
> *die rechte Hand 'raus,*   right hand out
> *'rein, 'raus, rein, raus,*
> *mach ein kleines Haus!*   points hands together as 'roof'
> *Dann kommt der Boogie Woogie*
> *und dreh dich um,*   turn round
> *und dann geht's wieder los!*
>
> *Boogie Woogie, Woogie.*
> *Boogie Woogie, Woogie.*
> *Boogie Woogie, Woogie.*
> *Links, rechts, links, rechts,*
> *Ra, Ra, Ra!*
>
> *Das rechte Bein 'rein,*   right leg in
> *das rechte Bein raus,*
> *'rein, raus, rein, raus,*
> *mach ein kleines Haus!*
> etc

Choose **tunes with lines which occur in every verse** with a **predictable pattern and inbuilt repetition.** This means that **all** children can sing along with the lines which are repeated. Another example is an adaptation of *If you're happy and you know it.*

For the first rehearsal, you can pick out the phrase with the accompanying action, here *'lach und klatsch in deine Händ'* which occurs three times. Encourage children to hum the start of the lines and join in with their bit at the end. Then add in the beginning *'wenn du froh bist'* which runs through each verse again and again, next *'kannst du lachen'* and finally *'und uns alle fröhlich machen.'* You now have all the components for each verse.

Wenn du froh bist

> *Wenn du froh bist,* **lach und klatsch in deine Händ'!**   clap your hands
> *Wenn du froh bist, lach und klatsch in deine Händ'!*
> *Wenn du froh bist, kannst du lachen*
> *und uns alle fröhlich machen!*
> *Wenn du froh bist, klatsch in deine Händ!*

> Tune: *If you're happy and you know it*

Do not feel that you must sing lots and lots of verses or complete songs. **Very short extracts** are just as effective, so you could stop with the first verse. A later run through might include building on what is already known *'wenn du froh bist, lach und . . .'* with the new 'nodding' movement *'nick mit deinem Kopf'* added in appropriately.

> *Wenn du froh bist,* **lach und nick mit deinem Kopf!**   ***nod your head***
> *Wenn du froh bist,* **lach und stampf mit deinem Fuß!**   ***stamp your feet***
> *Wenn du froh bist,* **lach und ruf 'Juchhe'!**   ***laugh and shout 'juchhe'***

During successive renderings, more and more members of the class should be able to move on from joining in with at least part of the verses to gradually building up to master the whole song.

USING PUBLISHED RESOURCES

There is an increasing repertoire of traditional and especially composed songs for young learners now available both on audio and video cassettes and in this section we suggest some we have found especially enjoyable. These constitute another valuable resource but just as we would not expect children to read and perform aloud at first sight, so we cannot expect them to sing along with a cassette without preparing the way.

AUDIOCASSETTES

The pre-listening stage is vitally important for you and the children. Don't forget to learn the words and tunes to any songs which are unfamiliar to you, before you teach them to the children! As you are doing so, look to see if there are any expressions or single lexical items that you can extract and teach using visuals in the usual way. Then there is less 'new' for children to learn when they come to listen to the cassette.

One of the advantages of a pre-recorded stimulus is that you can rewind and replay as many times as suits your own learners. However, many cassettes have extremely short songs which occur just once. Naturally, children typically want to sing anything they enjoy over and over again, so it is useful to record a favourite song several times in succession onto a tape of your own. Three times is usually about right! This prevents you having to rewind to and fro several times hunting for the 'right place'. Instead, the second or third version of the song comes up immediately. Don't forget to leave a blank pause in between the various songs though.

For instance, daily routine (and reflexive verbs!) can be rehearsed accompanied by a lively set of young children's voices using this song:

Je me lève	mime getting up
Je me lave	washing
Je me brosse les dents	cleaning teeth
Je m'habille	getting dressed
Je mange un petit croissant	eating breakfast
Je sors	going out the door
Je dis 'au revoir maman!'	waving goodbye
Encore!	(repeat)

An example of a medium length song is the traditional French song *Ainsi font les petites marionnettes* based on the workings of little puppets which is very popular. Play the recording and let pupils listen in order to become familiar with the tune and the general rhythmic pattern. Always be realistic about how much your class can manage. In this song the opening verse acts as a refrain with which children can join in to start off.

Les petites marionnettes

Ainsi font, font, font	move around jerkily as if on strings
Les petites marionnettes	of puppet
Ainsi font, font, font	refrain
Trois petits tours	turn round on the spot
Et puis s'en vont	march on spot

You will see that the expression '*trois petits tours*' has already been met in the context of the rhyme *Mes petites mains font tap! tap! tap!* featured in Part 1.

When the children are really familiar with the refrain, introduce one or all of the following verses. The chorus fits in between each time. Then say/sing each line and do the 'hands on hips' actions, building up bit by bit. If you are playing a cassette, turn the volume down for an increasing number of words as the class learns more. It is not necessary to sing everything at the first rehearsal.

Les mains aux côtés,	hands on hips
Marionnettes, marionnettes	swaying from side to side
Les mains aux côtés,	hands on hips
Marionnettes, sans desserrer	swaying from side to side
Ainsi font, font, font	(refrain)
Les petites marionnettes	
Ainsi font, font, font	
Trois petits tours	three little turns
Et puis s'en vont	
Les mains aux côtés	hands on hips
Sautez, sautez marionnettes	little jumps on the spot
Les mains aux côtés,	hands on hips
Marionnettes recommencez	little jumps on the spot

The following German song has a very rousing tune and good rythmn. Start by singing the chorus only and listening to the rest. Encourage the children to feel the beat through their bodies and keep in time.

54 — Young Pathfinder 6: *Let's join in! Rhymes, poems and songs*

ciLT

Manno manno mannomann!

Was ich kann, kann jeder sehn!	(listen to begin with)
Ich kann laufen, ich kann gehn.	run on spot
Ich kann sitzen und kann stehn	sit down, stand up
und mich schnell im Kreise drehn.	turn round on spot

Refrain:

Manno, manno, mannomann,	children clap
jeder zeigt uns, was er kann!	point at children round the group
Manno, manno, mannomann	
jeder zeigt uns, was er kann!	

Ich kann schleichen, wenn ich will,	children creep,
hocke wie ein Mäuschen still,	fingers on lips very quiet
liege faul wie'n Krokodil,	lay down still
rase wie ein Ball ins Ziel.	jump up, hands in the air

There are many more verses. They can be found in the collection *Denkt euch nur.*

These kind of songs are especially useful if you are not at ease singing unaccompanied as you can use the tape as a back up support. In the same way that spoken rhymes can be supported by text, so once children are familiar with oral versions of songs, you may wish to introduce some of your older or more able learners to them in their written form using similar techniques to those mentioned for the poems. This will especially be the case for these longer examples where the written word, along with the actions, will aid the task of memorisation.

Always remember to praise the children for moving to the music so well and for keeping to the beat. This next song builds up cumulatively. You can sketch each body part on a card and tell children to show the card as they hear their body part if they don't want to move themselves. If you run out of steam you can always listen to the last verses.

Die rechte Hand,	shake right hand starting
die rechte Hand fängt an	with very small movements
und bewegt sich.	increase
Die linke Hand,	shake left hand starting
die linke Hand,	with very small movements
seht her, sie bewegt sich,	
und damit fängt es an!	
Die rechte Hand, die linke Hand,	right hand, left hand
die rechte Hand, die linke Hand,	right hand, left hand
seht nur, wie schnell	shake faster and faster
man sich bewegen kann.	
Der rechte Arm,	right arm
der rechte Arm,	
fängt an und bewegt sich.	
Der linke Arm,	left arm
der linke Arm,	
seht her, er bewegt sich,	
und damit fängt es an!	
Die rechte Hand,	the hands from the first verse
die linke Hand,	plus
der rechte Arm,	the arms from the second verse
der linke Arm,	
seht nur wie schnell	
man sich bewegen kann!	
Der rechte Zeh	right toe . . .
Der rechte Fuß	right foot
Das rechte Bein	right leg

Die rechte Hand fängt an

You can make a **large A3 size songbook** from which individual children can choose the songs they wish the class to sing. Poster-sized versions of rhymes and songs can also be written out on sugar paper and form part of a display. These can be turned to, when there are a few moments available to say or sing.

As an alternative to moving with the whole body, you may like to use the same songs on cassette but turn a lively session into a more settled one by encouraging the children to hand-clap the beat or the rhythm to accompany a song they already know.

As the children's confidence increases, you can move on to play a 'traffic lights' game, usng a green and red 'lollipop' signal. When you show the green signal, the children clap and sing, but when you show the red signal they clap only and carry the song in their heads. Children need plenty of practice before they can do this well, but they all get there in the end.

Introduce musical instruments to help develop the sense of rhyme and rhythm, drums, bells, tambourines and shakers are useful.

One particularly appealing set of materials are the *Raconte et chante* books, each of which is accompanied by an audio cassette, which reworks a single song in a variety of ways. As well as a workbook for children, there are six huge storybooks which present portions of the text of the song on the left hand page and a colourful illustration on the right hand side. These are marvellous for reading to the children on the mat at story time. First, a single adult native speaker sings the text of the song which appears in the storybook accompanied by a simple melody and appropriate sound effects which fit the story, for example the sound of waves in the one entitled *A la mer.* This version includes key lines repeated several times, so that the children can focus for a while on a single page at a time before you turn over. Secondly, the song is read aloud as text by the native speaker, so if you are less confident, everyone can listen to both these spoken and sung versions straight from the cassette and enjoy the pictures which are a valuable talking point. Alternatively, this reading aloud can act as a model for the primary class teacher to imitate before undertaking the reading themselves. The lower case script is bold and so easy to read that you can point to each word at a time as it comes up in the song or indicate items in the pictures. As a third stage the song is sung with small gaps to enable the children to insert a single final word, e.g. *'mon seau est . . .'* (children sing *'vert'* in the gap). The fourth stage is similar, but a different set of words is missed out, usually a short phrase, which children insert at the appropriate point. Finally the melody is played alone, and children can sing without support from the native speaker once they have gained confidence.

All cultures have a host of nursery rhymes and songs, and as a comparison children could look at other illustrated collections of rhymes and songs in English and in the language of their home. Encourage children to bring in books from home and to teach their classmates rhymes they have learned in their first language.

VIDEO

Generally speaking it is probably advisable to use **video** as a source of something pleasurable to listen to and watch together. Listening is typically associated with testing and with spoken production, and it is important to remember the receptive nature of a lot of the listening we do, when we are listening for pleasure in a relaxed way.

As a source of fun in the classroom, karaoke videos are a good resource. You will find that these videos typically present the song firstly in audio form sung by native speakers and supported by colourful animated sequences. The song is then repeated as musical accompaniment only and the text given at the foot of the screen, providing an opportunity for learners to read the text and sing the song.

When the video- or audiocassette contains traditional songs and carols which you already know such as *Alouette, Sur le pont, Au clair de la lune* it is straightforward to join in and sing together. The videos then provide an appealing alternative means of presentation.

However, a number of the karaoke songs, because they are authentic, have fairly complex language, unusual vocabulary and to English ears, unfamiliar tunes. These are less easy to incorporate for active participation with primary learners, although they are pleasant for viewing and listening purposes. You may find that the graphics do not always support the meaning of the foreign language unambiguously and if you do want to use the highlighted text which appears on the screen to sing along with as a class, it will be essential to prepare your learners thoroughly for the text.

This pre-viewing stage is very necessary. Just as we would not expect children to be able to sing a song after hearing it once, so we must build in some intervening stages using all the strategies described so far. Do ensure the children know how to pronounce the words before you show the printed form, and remember that where they are following the words, listening to a new tune and attempting to join in, they will have more than enough to concentrate on.

If the printed word on screen is to be of support, children will need good reading skills. As there are intentionally no voice parts, you may find yourself singing to guide the children, so it is essential to be well prepared.

If your learners are not yet in a position to read the lyrics themselves, everyone can still watch the pictures and listen to the tune and the words and perhaps decide on a favourite song. Children like awarding points to different songs, voting on which one should have the highest score. More able readers will be able to 'follow' the song text in their heads as they listen to the cassette or watch the words coming on the video text. Everyone can comment on what they are seeing and hearing.

Whatever the stimulus, aural or visual or a combination, all pupils can create their own song books, built round illustrations and/or text as appropriate.

Cross curricular links with art and English can be made as children design a cover and evaluate the end product together; for example, they could consider what might be done differently another time — size, shape, cover, borders, pictures.

This forms a valuable record of the work they have done and is useful to go with them to their next school or into the next class.

Children can also mount displays featuring work based on the scenes from songs or rhymes including entries in English and other dialects.

Encourage learning by heart of familiar rhymes and songs to be performed to another class, in assembly or to parents, perhaps making use of the home made song books which can be taken home for practising.

You could also record the class reciting or singing some of the different rhymes and songs on tape.

TAKING THE LANGUAGE FURTHER

Write out the text of a favourite rhyme or song on card in large lower case letters with appropriate punctuation. Then cut out each verse line by line, in strips. More confident readers can then work in small groups to reassemble chunks of text in the right order, using capital letters at the start of sentences, full stops and punctuation, word and letter recognition together with a thorough prior knowledge of the rhyme.

If appropriate, the sequencing task can be carried out using a word processor. You would need to prepare the original text in a large clear font and jumble the order of the lines. Working in twos or threes, pupils can then be shown how to move pieces of text around using 'cut' and 'paste' commands. Alternatively, a text manipulation package such as *Fun with Texts* could be used. Different files would be required for children of differing abilities.

As an extension, you can make a cloze text by of a familiar song by removing/blanking out one or two key words and letting pupils fill in the gaps. Use large lower case letters with big gaps. If you choose concrete nouns, pupils can **draw in the gaps rather than write.**

As a next step, they can **write** the missing words. As support, provide a list of words on the worksheet from which pupils can choose. You can give clues by putting the same number of dashes in the gaps as matches the number of letters in the word rather than an empty gap. You can add further support by giving the initial letter of the word required.

This kind of task develops the skills initiated earlier with spelling and alphabet work, when **individual letters** were omitted from well-known words. Now learners have progressed to **replacing words or even short meaningful phrases.**

USING RHYMES AND SONGS FOR CREATIVE WRITING

In Part 1 we indicated how young learners could contribute to the creation of new songs by choosing toys from the appropriate piles. Now we include a simple rhyme in German presented in text form for children to substitute their own food and drink items.

Ich
habe . . .

Ich habe Hunger, Hunger, Hunger,
habe Hunger, Hunger, Hunger,
habe Hunger, Hunger, Hunger,
habe Durst!

Wo bleibt das **Essen, Essen, Essen,**
bleibt das Essen, Essen, Essen,
bleibt das Essen, Essen, Essen,
bleibt **die Wurst***?*

Using the same idea of counting syllables, the word '*Essen*' in the second verse could be changed to: '*Wo bleibt der Honig/der Käse/der Kaffee/die Pizza/die Suppe/die Cola/das Schnitzel/das Müsli/das Wasser*', etc and the one syllable '*Wurst*' be changed to '*Milch, Saft*', etc.

The same poem, because of its very limited range of vocabulary, is also suitable for lower achieving pupils to copywrite.

Le chocolat

Le chocolat, moi, j'aime ça
Ça fait des moustaches comme Papa
Le pain, le beurre, la confiture
Ça colle aux doigts comme la peinture!

Here is a very short French poem also on the food theme. Again children can replace their own food and drink items for the underlined French ones. They can also combine to suggest an alternative last line depending on the words they come up with.

A restful song for practising shopping dialogues is as follows. It has a steady tune which children can follow easily and lends itself to children singing in groups, according to the speakers in the various verses. Children can then use it as a model for their own role play dialogues substituting the underlined words. Give them various possibilities for the other flavours. They can also pretend to be shopkeepers selling different products, and request items which match their choice of shopkeeper.

60 — Young Pathfinder 6: *Let's join in! Rhymes, poems and songs*

ciLT

Moi, je vends des glaces
Dans le grand marché
Abricot banane
Chocolat café
Ah bonjour, ma fille
Qu'est-ce que tu voudrais?
Je voudrais une vanille
Monsieur s'il vous plaît

Moi, je vends des glaces
Dans le grand marché
Abricot banane
Chocolat café
Ah bonjour, ma fille
Qu'est-ce que tu voudrais?
Je voudrais une praline
Monsieur s'il vous plaît

■ DEVELOPING PUPIL LANGUAGE BY MEANS OF HOME-MADE SONGS

In Part 1 we focused on adapting well-known tunes of both English and foreign origin for the purposes of practising simple structures and in particular on teacher use of the target language to give instructions and praise. We now turn to **pupil language.**

There will be occasions when your pupils will be playing games, perhaps at their tables in small groups. These may be simple board or card games and is is particularly appropriate to teach some of the 'game playing' language in the same way that we have suggested for classroom language. Take a well-known tune such as *Sur le pont d'Avignon.* Like many songs, this is one which children get to know from all sorts of sources and is one for joining in with. Both boys and girls in the class can take it in turn to do the actions for each verse as appropriate.

<table>
<tr><td>Tune:
Sur le pont
d'Avignon</td><td>Sur le pont d'Avignon
On y danse
On y danse
Sur le Pont d'Avignon
On y danse
Tous en rond</td></tr>
</table>

Les beaux messieurs font comme ça	bow
Et puis encore comme ça	bow again
Les belles dames font comme ça	curtsey
Et puis encore comme ça	curtsey again
Les militaires font comme ça	salute
Et puis encore comme ça	salute again

We have highlighted the first verse, because if you take that only, you can change it to become:

Qui commence? C'est à qui?
C'est à toi
C'est à toi
Qui commence? C'est à qui?
C'est à toi!
Tu commences!

Note how we have tried to **keep to the same pattern of repeats as the original**, so *'c'est toi, c'est à toi'* reflects the *'on y danse, on y danse'* from the original and the *'sur le pont d'Avignon'* which occurs twice is mirrored by the *'Qui commence? C'est à qui?'* Another verse might be adapted for playing a board game as follows:

Tune: *Sur le pont* *d'Avignon*

A la case départ
Lance le dé
Lance le dé
A la case départ
Lance le dé
Avance avance!

Or you could adapt that old favourite, *Frère Jacques!*

Tune: *Frère Jacques*

C'est à qui?
C'est à qui?
C'est mon tour
C'est ton tour
Il ne faut pas tricher
Il ne faut pas tricher
J'ai gagné!
J'ai gagné!

Another tune you can adapt, this time of English origin, is *Three blind mice.*

Tune: *Three blind mice*

Wer fängt an?
Wer fängt an?
[Mark] du fängst an!
Nimm den Würfel und würfle!
Nimm den Würfel und würfle!
Du fängst an!

Wer ist dran?
Wer ist dran?
Du bist dran!
Eine Sechs! Noch einmal würfeln!
Eine Sechs! Noch einmal würfeln!
Du bist dran!

Conclusion

Rhymes, poems, tongue twisters and song texts learnt as a child often stay with us for the rest of our lives and are well worth the time spent on them. Young children can be drawn into the foreign language by their curiosity for sounds, rhythm and pattern, especially when these are accompanied by actions or visual stimuli.

Songs and rhymes provide a context which allows children to learn 'chunks' of language in a comfortable way, giving them an intuitive awareness of the rhythm of the spoken language and of its syntax and intonation.

Many people find themselves humming familiar tunes, and each time the learner does this it is an opportunity for the words to be practised and listened to again and again, even if it is only 'inside one's head'. Therefore we can say that music or rhythm inside the learner's head gives frequent exposure to the foreign language, even when the learner is not in the classroom. This kind of exposure from an early age is invaluable in the UK context, as there is little or no exposure to foreign languages through the medium of pop music, TV or films in the way that there is exposure to English in other parts of the world.

By learning songs and rhymes a child can acquire a wealth of linguistic knowledge, and the teacher can then tap into this knowledge by making links with discrete language points when they are taught in other contexts. In this way, songs and rhymes can be used not only as a reinforcement to learning but as a point of departure from which to take the child further.

Rhymes and songs have their own special context for language learning, it is possible that some of those children who lack the confidence 'to be themselves' when participating in routine speaking and listening sequences can sometimes lose such inhibitions and confidently join in the reciting or singing of a rhyme or song in chorus with their friends. Thus the rhymes and songs are vehicles which can permit learners to shape their mouths and utter foreign sounds when they might otherwise not have wished to do so. Their use can build confidence and self esteem, as in saying a rhyme the child can imagine herself to be following a script unlike other kinds of speaking and listening routines where the learner might feel embarrassed or exposed by the possibility of not knowing the words. The learner is allowed to utter the spoken word with a high degree of fluency, accuracy and rhythm.

If our foreign language learners can be accustomed to developing fluency and accuracy from an early age through songs and rhymes and to feel successful as 'performers' in the foreign language, we hope that positive attitudes will be formed which will motivate the learner to project this early feeling of success onto the whole range of language activities.

Of course it has not been possible to say everything that could be said in this Young Pathfinder but we hope you will enjoy reciting and singing and become as enthusiastic about finger and action rhymes and songs as we are!

Useful sources

FRENCH

Chante en français (songbook + cassette) from La Jolie Ronde Educational, 33 Longacre Road, Bingham, Nottingham NG13 8AF

Entre dans la ronde (songbook + cassette) from La Jolie Ronde (see above)

Le français, c'est facile from John Murray Publishers, 50 Albemarle Street, London W1X 4BD

Les petits Lascars coffret comptines 1 and 2 from Didier*

Raconte et chante: 6 books and cassettes (*A la mer, Les amis de la ferme, Anniversaire de la ferme, Plic — plic — tombe la pluie, Un pique nique, Monsieur l'arbre et la petite fille*) available separately from the European Language Institute (ELI)*

GERMAN

Alle Affen und Giraffen, cassette and songbook (rubrics in German) from Verlag für Deutsch*

Denkt euch nur, der Frosch war krank, cassette and songbook from Menschenkinder Verlag*

Komm mit! Early steps in German, two cassettes from Goethe-Institut, Manchester. Tel: 0161 237 1077

Wer Wie Was songbook from Gilde Verlag*

VIDEOS

Des chansons pour la maternelle by M. Ficelle from Pop English Creations*

Jeux de doigts from La Jolie Ronde Educational (see above)

Le Karaoke de Noël, French Christmas songs from ELI*

Mon âne no. 1 and no. 2, chansons traditionnelles sous-titrées, from Production Distribution Folimage, 6, Rue Jean Bertin, F-26000, Valence France. Tel: +334 75 43 60 30. Fax: +334 75 43 06 92

Voilà le Karaoke bleu, traditional French songs from ELI*

Voilà le Karaoke rouge, traditional French songs from ELI*

* available from European Schoolbooks. Tel: 01242 245 252

Acknowledgements

The publishers and authors would like to thank the following for their permission to reproduce materials in this Young Pathfinder:

La Jolie Ronde, LJR Educational, 33 Long Acre, Bingham, Nottingham, NG13 8AF.
Tel: 01949 839 715

p4 *Bonjour Papa*
p5 *Voici ma main* (all from *Entre dans la ronde*)
p23 *Nounours touche le nez*
p32 *Sic au lit* (from *Chante en français*)

Living and Learning Ltd, 527 Pembroke Avenue, Waterbeach, Cambridgeshire, CB5 9QP.
Tel: 01223 864 886

p8 *Les sept jours de la semaine*
p53 *Je me lève* (from *French start*, Teresa Scibor, Club Tricolore, available from Early Learning Centres)

Le Club Français, 18/19 High Street, Twyford, Winchester, SO21 1RF (membership includes club cassette and songbook)

p51 *Le Gouzi-gouzi*

Mary Glasgow Publications, Stanley Thornes Publishers Ltd, Ellenborough House, Wellington Street, Cheltenham, Gloucester, GL50 1YW. Tel: 01242 228 888

p49 *Quelle est le date de ton anniversaire?*
p61 *Moi, je vends des glaces dans le grand marché* (from *Un kilo de chansons* by Jasper Kay)

Gilde Verlag (distributed in UK by European Schoolbooks. Tel: 01242 245 252)

p18 *Der Regenbogen komm und schau* (from *Wer Wie Was* songbook by Manfred Wahl)

Menschenkinder verlag (distributed in UK by European Schoolbooks. Tel: 01242 245 252)

p55 *Manno manno mannomann* (both from *Denkt euch nur, der Frosch war krank*
p56 *Die rechte Hand* by Rolf Krenzer, music: Anke Jocker)

Goethe-Institut, Manchester. Tel: 0161 237 1077

p23 *Ein großer Hund eine kleine Katze*
p32 *Eins, zwei, Polizei*

66 — Young Pathfinder 6: *Let's join in! Rhymes, poems and songs*

C*i*LT